How to Make

Millions from Apps

By Benjamin Bressington

Fast track your app success with the secrets of how I went from zero to over 150 apps in six months with no coding, programming or design skills.

rev 08.02.11

Tigga Studios LLC

9190 Double Diamond Pkwy, Ste 5573, Reno, NV, USA, 89521

www.TiggaStudios.com

More Information www.HowToMakeMillionsFromApps.com

Table of Contents

Introduction

Mobile apps are all the rage for users of all ages, and across all walks of life. Applications have replaced boring old software programs with fun, portable, and extremely useful applications that can be opened and used on a wide variety of mobile devices.

See that guy sitting next to you at the airport working on his iPad? Or the teenager who is playing a game on her mobile device while waiting for the bus? Chances are good that both of them – and millions of other individuals – are using mobile apps.

Whether they are communicating with other mobile users (with SMS text apps like Handcent); writing up documents (on Documents to Go); playing Angry Birds (you got it – on Angry Birds); or reading the news (on USA Today or the New York Times), people around the world have caught onto the value of apps.

Credit the 300-pound gorilla Apple with starting the trend. For before the Apple app store came about the general consumer didn't know an Angry Bird from a Happy Bird. They had no idea what type of fun, productive lives they could be living with the help of mobile applications, and they certainly didn't realize that a $600 tablet computer could serve as a virtual mother ship for pretty much all of the "software" that was once housed on their memory-intensive desktop computers.

Fast-forward to 2012 and the app revolution has both begun and taken off like a skyrocket. Trust me on this one. I certainly wouldn't be writing this book if it hadn't (maybe I'd be writing about how to develop memory-hogging software programs or something…but who knows?). **Now is the time for all current and potential app developers to stand at attention and start cashing in on a trend that's sure to be in place for years.** Consumers' appetites for apps are simply insatiable, so why shouldn't you play a part in satisfying them by creating and selling your own cool and useful apps?

I will show you how to do that – and more – in this book. You'll learn about the top app distribution channels, find out where to get the best ideas for apps, and hear how the "improving on what's already out there" strategy can serve you well as a developer. We'll also help you develop your first scope document, form your development team, and get your app published.

Shhh…Insider App Secret!

To make it even easier for you I have created templates and resources available in the members' area for this book at www.howtomakemillionsfromapps.com/bookmember. *These resources and bonuses are free and will help you connect with other like-minded app publishers.*

We'll also cover important topics like app marketing, app promotion, and monetization. We'll give you top strategies and show you how others are already generating significant revenues with their apps. Finally, you'll learn why you should create a portfolio of apps (and not just a single product) and how to sell your company when the time is right.

The best part is that you will discover all of these secrets without the need for coding, programming, or design knowledge. I know that I still consider that to be magic, but I will share with you how you can attain this magic on even the smallest of budgets.

In the first chapter we'll introduce you to the marketplace and the key players, and show you why mobile apps are such a great opportunity. Are you ready to learn? Flip over to the next page and let's get started.

Chapter One:

Why Mobile Apps?

If you aren't convinced that there's a market for apps, check this single statistic from research group Flurry Analytics: 1.2 billion apps were downloaded during the holiday week from December 25-31, 2011. That's <u>one single week's worth of apps!</u> Compound that number across an entire year and the resulting number is simply astounding (I'll let you handle that – I don't think my calculator even has enough digits to do that kind of math problem, but you get the point – it's a big number).

Here are a few more statistics to show you what a great opportunity you have in app development:

- ✓ Since 2007, more than 500 million iOS and Android smartphones and tablets have been activated.
- ✓ By the end of 2012, the cumulative number of iOS and Android devices activated will surge past 1 billion.
- ✓ According to research firm IDC, over 800 million PCs were sold between 1981 and 2000, making the rate of iOS and Android smart device adoption more than four times faster than that of personal computers.
- ✓ Flurry reports that smartphone and tablet users spend over an hour and a half of their day using applications.
- ✓ Meanwhile, average time spent on the Web has shrunk, from 74 minutes to 72 minutes (from June 2011 to present).
- ✓ App growth is being driven by an increase in the number of sessions, as opposed to longer session lengths, according to Flurry. *That means consumers are using their apps more frequently.*

So that's the marketplace. Pretty impressive, right?

There is another market that influences the apps marketplace and that is gaming. Collectively, the planet is now spending more than 3 billion hours a week gaming. That is a very large number and it is growing every week, to the point that businesses are looking to game designers to apply game strategies to their marketing campaigns. This is the process of "gamification," and it involves creating something addictive, engaging and rewarding to users.

Here are some relevant statistics from the Entertainment Software Association's annual study of game players. This is the largest and most widely respected market research report of its kind:

- ✓ 69 percent of all heads of households play computer or video games.
- ✓ 97 percent of youth play computer and video games.
- ✓ 40 percent of all gamers are women.
- ✓ One out of four gamers is over the age of fifty.
- ✓ The average game player is thirty-five years old and has been playing for twelve years.

If you can pick up on trends in the market you can create apps to cater for these segments of the apps market. Pick your battles and select niches that you can work in. You are not going to dominate the entire games market because it is so diversified and segmented, but you can dominate various sub-segments of the market.

Now it's time to look at the key players and break them down in a way that helps you understand exactly what you'll be working with.

Working With App Markets

Several key players have made their mark on the mobile application space. Apple, Android, and Amazon are a few of the biggest names. There are also myriad smaller markets that may not have the marquee names out front, but they can add dollars to your annual business revenues.

Shhh…Insider App Secret!

There are pros and cons to using each app platform, and there are myriad cross-platform tools at your avail. These tools will allow you to design your applications to run on multiple platforms without having to redesign your app for each individual target market (we'll explore this strategy in depth later in this book).

The key players in the app market, and the smaller platforms, will serve as your business distribution channels. They provide the storefronts where users worldwide visit to browse through, buy, and download the latest and greatest mobile applications. That's your bread and butter so it's important that you know which ones are at your avail and how they work (we'll go over them in the next section.)

One of the concepts I want you to understand is that each app marketplace is its own "ecosystem." Within the ecosystems are subcultures that can be profit centers for your business. For example, Apple IOS is available for the iPhone, iPad, and iPod touch. Those are the three app markets within Apple iOS that you can cater too. Each subculture comes its own rules (much like every country has it own rules).

The app markets are separate from each other but can be connected to one another to make your app viral. You will be amazed at the trends you can see in app stores outside the USA and at the profitability you can attain by catering to these markets. The same concept can be expanded to Android, Windows phone, Amazon, the Nook, and even the evolution of HTML5. I personally believe that HTML 5 is in its infancy and that you don't need to worry about it until at least 2015. What you should be catering to is Apple IOS and Android, followed by Amazon then Windows phone.

As you explore your distribution options you should know that some developers focus tightly on a single application market, such as the Android Market. These developers earn respectable profits with their single-market approach, but others earn even more by spreading their wings across other channels.

The good news is that you don't have to focus on multiple platforms to make money from apps. You can generate revenues by focusing on a single platform – in fact, that's how you should get started anyway. Instead of spreading yourself too thin right out of the gate, take the time to learn, understand, and work with a single platform first. Then take it from there.

Shhh…Insider App Secret!

I want to make it clear: **you do not need any coding, programming or design experience to make your apps and I even recommend that you do not worry about learning it.** I   have published over 150 apps and I have no coding, programming and design skills at all even to this very day. What I do know how to do well is hire and inspire a team to work on my projects quickly, and to create low-cost apps that make money. This is the secret that I want to share with you in this book. Along with providing you with the tools and resources to fast track your success (see the bonus section and the resource area in the member's only area on the website). My goal is to fast track your app success and increase your app revenues.

Once you've developed several applications you can grow your market share by exploring additional distribution channels (i.e., app markets and platforms) for your products. Just like Walmart gains market share by opening new stores in rural areas, you can leverage your successful apps across new platforms in order to generate higher income levels.

The Big Two: Players in the App Market

The top distribution channels for mobile applications right now are Apple IOS and the Android marketplace.

Apple https://developer.apple.com/

The 300-pound gorilla in the app space, Apple has two main application distribution portals. One is a mobile IOS developer platform and the other is a MAC OS developer platform. Here's how these two platforms work:

> The Apple IOS developer platform link to access more information about this program is here: http://developer.apple.com/programs/ios/

Using this program you pay an annual fee to Apple to join the IOS developer program. When you sign up you'll gain access to the IOS SDK, where you can start developing your IOS applications for the iPad, iPhone, and iPod touch.

Even if you are employing coders or developers you will need your own developer account for when you actually publish your apps in the App Store (I'll discuss this in more depth later in this book). If you want to get paid you need to publish to your own developer account.

The Mac App Store is a new way for people to download software directly to their machines without having to purchase a CD or DVD. This store and its functionalities represent the future of software delivery and clearly illustrate how multiple platforms are now facilitating this distribution.

Shhh...Insider App Secret!

When you're expanding your marketplace, don't forget about your cross-platform users. iPhone users, for example, will interact differently with your app than someone who is using a Macbook. Factor this issue in when you're designing and developing your apps and be sure to test them out on different platforms.

Android

http://market.android.com/publish

The Android marketplace is a new, adaptive platform that's extremely popular among handset users. But it's not a replica of the Apple app store. There is a slight difference in the way that users interact on the app platforms themselves. (I personally believe that the Android platform will become a major competitor and player to the Apple IOS platform in 2012, and that in the long term catering to this market will be very important for any developer.)

Android gained prowess rather quickly because of its relationship with Google. The Android marketplace is integrated into the Google network and, as such, caters to hundreds of millions of people worldwide. Here's how the Android market works:

There are different Android devices in use and their numbers grow every month. This is an important point for developers who must incorporate these elements and integrations into their application design. Differences in hardware, screen resolutions, SDK's on the devices, tablets all operate uniquely as compared to the Apple IOS SDK.

With the current progress being made by Google checkout and Google wallet, the Android's purchasing process is in a stage of rapid, continual improvement. I expect the platform to expand further when technologies like near field communication (NFC) become commonplace. NFC technologies allow for mobile payment processing using the swipe of your mobile phone instead of a credit card. Such technologies hold huge potential and are sure to change the way consumers pay for their apps and other purchases in the near future.

It's important to note that there are many distribution channels for Android apps. From these channels, people can download your applications (unlike the Apple IOS platform, where they can only download your app through iTunes or via the app store). Knowing this, you'll want to create your Android apps in a way that caters to many different distribution channels – or, as many of them as possible – in order to increase your app's exposure.

Android has been evolving rapidly but is set to explode in 2012 for these primary reasons:

1. The cost of handsets and devices is much cheaper than that any other platform hardware. You can now purchase Android hardware under $100 (compared to

iPhones and iPads, which are $199 and up).

2. Other manufacturers are launching phone models that run the Android platform (for example, Nokia). There will be a bigger variety of handsets and tablets focused at the low end of the consumer market.

These two factors – along with the software improvements of the Android operating system – are making Android a profitable platform that developers must take seriously. Whatever you can make (or already are making) on Apple iOS right now is minimal when compared to what will be possible over the next few years with Android users.

Think of this app marketplace as a global ecosystem that is influenced by many factors, such as the average disposable income or available telephone company call and data plans. These all vary from country to country, which means adoption rates are significantly different in each country. When you are thinking of your app distribution consider which users and market segments you want to cater too.

Other Leaders in the App Market

Apple and Android aren't the only two kids playing in the app pool right now. Here are a few others that you should know about:

Amazon App Store Developer Program
https://developer.amazon.com

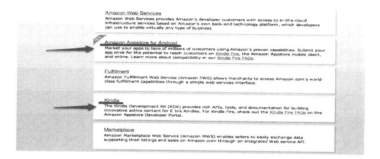

Leave it to Amazon to get its foot in the door with the very hot, popular app craze. This company hasn't missed out on any corner of the Web revenue market, and it certainly wasn't going to let this opportunity pass it by!

As Amazon moves into app stores and mobile marketplaces you will see the collective power of this Internet behemoth on the app distribution market. With the introduction of the Kindle Fire (during the fourth quarter of 2011), and other mobile devices running the Amazon operating system, now is the time to think about how you can gain exposure to tens of millions of customers who are already plugged into and buying from the Amazon network.

Shhh...Insider App Secret!

The Amazon Kindle marketplace is proving to be profitable for developers as a distribution

channel. But, you need to ensure your application is suitable for this marketplace. If you are looking for ideas, creating applications around books, or interactive, story-based games is extremely popular and profitable.

Adobe Air Platform http://www.adobe.com/products/air.html

This is an interesting marketplace for the expansion of web-based applications. The Adobe Air Platform allows you to build standalone applications and publish a cross-platform app that reaches a diverse audience. Devices covered include Android, Blackberry, personal computers, and televisions.

As you can imagine, Adobe pushes developers to think differently about the way they create and design their app codes. Because so many different devices can interact with the apps, it can be extremely cost-effective to create an app using the Adobe Air Platform. The distribution possibilities are huge if you're willing to put the time into developing apps that can reach a multitude of devices.

Windows Mobile

http://msdn.microsoft.com/en-us/windowsmobile

The Windows mobile platform allows you to create apps for any Windows compatible devices. I expect this market to expand as more handsets are released with the Windows-based platform (after all, Windows is an undisputed market leader in operating systems). This is not a platform that you should dismiss when assessing which marketplaces to cater to. However, just like the other small platforms mentioned in this chapter, understand that you will need to create code specifically for this operating system (and the devices that use it).

Shhh…Insider App Secret!

Did you know that Nokia is committed to making the Windows OS one of the top three mobile operating systems? This is not something to take lightly when you are considering how to build your apps business. You should have a Windows OS strategy in your expansion plan. Don't dismiss Nokia's market share in different countries around the world, as you can collect good profits by catering to this distribution channel. Don't wait for the masses to act. Get in early and ride this wave all the way to the bank.

BlackBerry

http://us.blackberry.com/developers

The BlackBerry marketplace is one of the smallest but it caters to an extremely loyal user base that's willing to pay money for the apps that help them work smarter, better, and faster (this is a market of business owners, after all).

Top app developers in the BlackBerry marketplace are racking up hundreds of thousand of dollars per year from the apps they've developed in this marketplace. If you have quality apps that are performing well on other platforms you may find the smaller BlackBerry market to be a solid revenue generator.

If you want to target the BlackBerry handset OS and the BlackBerry playbook OS you can develop your apps through the HTML 5 platform. This will allow you to dramatically increase your app development and publication capabilities. HTML 5 is a new standard in developing multimedia that also allows for cross-platform development. There are many APIs and integration platforms that allow you to develop native and web-based apps using HTML 5.

Facebook

This popular social networking site has its own ecosystem of applications and mobile applications that have spawned companies like social network game developer Zynga, which generates hundreds of millions of dollars a year from game portfolios.

The Facebook ecosystem also provides for a new world of multiplayer desktop-based and mobile device-based games. Many companies do very well in the Facebook ecosystem. However, they haven't been able to replicate that success in the mobile device market.

Facebook changes its rules and terms of play frequently. This is a key consideration when you are catering to this marketplace. You may find yourself updating and upgrading your apps based on Facebook's whims.

Shhh...Insider App Secret!

You can greatly benefit by integrating into your app design social media technologies that facilitate "sharing" amongst users. By allowing users to compete and involve their friends your game play will increase.

More to Come

Many new mobile application channels are being created every year. There are some that you may never use or cater to, but for those developers who are serious about increasing their market share and generating annual, ongoing profits from mobile applications, the opportunities abound.

As you assess the various app platforms at your avail it's important to understand that every one of them will cost money to publish your apps on. Think about this as you come up with a plan for approaching these markets and for leveraging your development dollars and time across as many as possible.

They're always ways to leverage and maximize your development costs by using cross-platform publishing tools, but they too come with their own set of pros and cons. If you're just getting started I suggest you kick off your strategy by creating apps for the Apple platform, and then expand your reach from there.

Don't worry about competition in the mobile app marketplace. Unlike the Facebook application marketplace, one company will not dominate the mobile application marketplace. The mobile marketplace is far too large and every platform has its own ecosystem within every country and language.

The mobile marketplace will have several major players who are big in certain countries or platforms. But it will not have one major player that dominates all. You will see multiple, big publishers, all of which will have a certain market share. Independent developers like you will total a certain market share as well, so there will always be room for you in the app marketplace.

I am certain you will see an increase in larger companies acquiring smaller app publishers or developers like you to add to their portfolios. I believe you will even see mutual funds and financial institutions investing in app publishers, due to the returns generated by these firms. Right now the app marketplace is a wild west that you can compare to the dotcom world back in the late 1990's. No one knows who is going to be the next app millionaire, but we all know that you'll have to be publishing apps in order to be eligible for that title!

Key Points to Remember from Chapter One

✓ The key players in the app market and the smaller platforms will serve as your business distribution channels.

✓ Apple has two main application distribution portals: the mobile IOS developer platform and the MAC OS developer platform.

✓ There are many distribution channels for Android apps.

✓ Developing your apps through the HTML 5 platform will allow you to dramatically increase your app development and publication capabilities.

✓ Every app platform will cost money to publish your apps on.

✓ You can leverage and maximize your development costs by using cross-platform publishing tools.

Chapter Two:

Brainstorming Great App Ideas

Great app ideas are all around you. In fact, I'd bet money on the fact that at some point you've said to yourself, "Wow, this would make a great app!" Maybe it was when you were facing your own struggle with technology, grappling with an everyday issue, or wishing beyond all hope that someone would create a mobile phone game that actually engaged your interest and time.

You can fill those gaps by developing the apps that not only meet your own needs, but that appeal to a broad audience of folks who share your frustrations and desires.

The right app starts with the right idea. It is much easier than most people think and it really needs to be as simple as possible so any child can work it out without requiring instructions. It should be as solid and concise as possible (saying you're going to develop the next hot mobile game won't work – you have to be specific and narrow in your scope) and it should meet at least one of the following rules:

- ✓ **My app solves a unique problem:** We all struggle with weight problems, nutritional issues, relationship strains, and work issues. What kind of app can you come up with that addresses one of these problems in a very specific way? Figure out what pressing issues your target audience is dealing with and then come up with an app that helps ease the pain.
- ✓ **My app serves a specific niche audience:** Your first goal should be universal appeal but, when that's not possible, you can always whittle your efforts down to one

specific niche. Let's say you're a triathlete (those crazy buggers that swim, bike, and run for inordinate lengths of time to test their mettle) who knows that there's no app for logging and charting your many training hours. Fill the niche with your own app that helps your fellow athletes (and even those outside of your sport) keep track of their progress.

✓ **My app picks up where other apps leave off:** No need to reinvent the wheel here. Let's say you've been using an app that has obvious flaws and that's lacking key features. That's your cue to build a better mousetrap that fills the gaps where your competition left off.

✓ **My app engages users with interactivity:** The best apps are the ones that keep users engaged for hours on end. We know that's not always possible, but you should strive to create something that your users don't close within a minute because they're bored with it. Get them involved, keep them up to date, and make them want to come back for more.

Of course there are other ways to measure the success of an app, but if yours comfortably falls into one or more of the four categories listed above, then you just may have a winner on your hands.

Shhh...Insider App Secret!

If you are building a game, you need to build a challenge into it. People need to fail, and you need to make failing fun and exciting. If you can make failing fun you will have an addictive game. Part of a game's success is the difficulty ratings and allowing players to fail and experience the *fiero* and *nache* emotions. (Check out M.I.N.D Labs fun failure research for more information about the concept of "fun failing" and how you can build this into your games.)

You'll hear this a few times throughout this book because it definitely bears repeating: **your app doesn't have to be original**. The proof lies in apps like Quickoffice, a productivity tool for viewing and editing Microsoft documents. Throughout 2011 this app – which came to be when its developer realized that Microsoft wasn't going to jump on the iPad bandwagon and start making compatible apps for the device – stayed on the list of top three grossing applications. Quickoffice's total sales topped $30 million and were expected to grow by another 50 percent in 2012. Those sales were generated from a concept based on a popular office software suite that's existed for decades. Who can argue with those numbers?

Once your creative juices start to flow your great app ideas will start coming to you in your sleep. Much like a serial entrepreneur can't stop scribbling new business ideas on his or her cocktail napkins, you'll be rushing to your computer or notepad on a regular basis in an effort to capture your new ideas.

My biggest challenge is getting all of my great app ideas recorded, and quickly. I get ideas when talking to friends over coffee and hearing them talk about the apps that they use, and the ones that they wish someone would develop (I like the latter the best!).

Shhh...Insider App Secret!

Guess what? You don't need a unique app idea to make a lot of money in this business. In fact, there are very full categories of apps where the top offerings all do very well financially. So don't be discouraged if you can't come up with a completely unique solution to a problem or demand. Simply take what's out there already and make it better!

In this book you'll find plenty of resources and ideas that you can use to start developing your own app ideas. As you consider the possibilities remember that the most successful apps are based on very simple ideas (does it seriously get any more basic than Angry Birds and Tiny Zoo – both of which rank as top grossing iPad apps?).

Shhh…Insider App Secret!

If you are struggling with creating an app idea don't worry. I have created over two hours of step-by-step video lessons where I share the exact steps that I take to create hundreds of app ideas. I will show you how to never worry about an idea for an app ever again! Check out the App Success System at http://www.AppSuccessSystem.com

Put simply, a successful app is one that people download and pay for, and that creates a steady revenue stream for its owner. Nowhere does it say that an app has to be complicated or original to achieve those goals.

What an app <u>must</u> do is target an audience of users who will pay for it. As a developer, it's important to keep this in mind and to understand how these customers are going to use your app. The more clarity you have in the early stages of development the better your end result will be.

One of the best ways to get started when creating your apps is to check out what's already popular. This is a fairly simple exercise as there are several places online that regularly rank the top paid apps currently on the market. If you use the Apple or Android market you can find these lists by accessing the market and hitting the "top charts" button on your device.

Pay attention to the paid apps, but don't ignore the free ones as you may see an opportunity to take a best-selling app in that category into the "paid" realm by improving upon what's already out there. Free apps will be downloaded ten times more than paid apps. I personally make great profits from free apps through advertising or in-app-purchases.

A review of the top 25 charts should prime your imagination and get you thinking about what types of apps you'd like to develop. If you're going to be "borrowing" ideas from another source be sure to put your own spin on them to avoid copyright infringement issues. (This is an area that you may want to get legal advice on down the road.)

Investigating the Top Apps

Now let's take a closer look at how you can use the top app charts to your advantage. Some of the best ways to view the current top 25 apps is actually not from within the iTunes App Store, but instead from other online websites.

Your ultimate goal should be to get your own app (or apps) onto these charts. There are major benefits to having this happen. First, it's the only way to ensure that your app goes viral with the possibility of millions of downloads. I'll discuss marketing strategies for getting to this point in a later chapter, but for now it's just important to understand that apps that are currently in the Top 25 are the ones you ultimately want to be competing against.

In some cases the apps on the lists will change on a daily basis. By understanding movements in the top 100 apps at any given time you'll be able to rapidly build apps that can capitalize on the opportunities that are out there.

Apple Apps Store Chart

Once you load iTunes and visit the App Store you'll see multiple charts ranking the top apps across various categories. You can see what's popular right now, track the up-and-coming apps, and see which programs have fallen off the charts. Pay particular attention to the top-grossing charts (the ones that Quickoffice – mentioned earlier in this chapter – tends to dominate by staying in first, second, or third place).

The top grossing charts show which apps that are making the most money right now. The apps that are ranked may offer a free download, and then demand some type of payment from users who want to access their "full" versions, or that want to enjoy the apps without the pop-up advertisement (these are "advertising-free" apps). It's important to educate yourself on exactly how these apps are generating revenues for their owners, and then replicate some or all of their successful techniques.

Remember that you'll always get more downloads when your app is free than if you command an upfront fee for the download. The trick will be to create an offer that users can't refuse by giving them something free at the outset, and then asking them to pay for an upgraded version. I'll give you a lot of ideas for making money from free apps in a later chapter, but for now let's just focus on some excellent app creation ideas.

New and Noteworthy

The "new and noteworthy" category lists some of the newest

apps that have been published in the App Store, and that are already doing very well. Use this list to get some ideas for games or apps that range from the very simple to the extremely complex.

Shhh....Insider App Secret!

Apple loves games that are beautifully designed and that appeal to discerning gamers that enjoy a challenge. Time should be taken with the details within the game, particularly if you want it to do well in the App Store. By taking the time to create a quality, highly designed app with Zen-like details you will increase the chances of your app being featured in the Apple "staff pick" categories.

As you look over the various lists of best-selling apps, pay attention to whether they are meant for use on the iPhone, iPad, or both. Not all apps cater to both devices; some are designed specifically for one or the other. This is a consideration that you'll want to work through before you start the development phase, as it will affect the way you handle the process, and the final outcome.

You may also want to look deeper into the categories that are available within the Apple App Store to get an idea of which apps target the markets that you want to go after. If, for example, your goal is to make an app that helps users count their daily calories and chart their weight loss progress, look at what's already out there in that category <u>before</u> you start developing. This type of market research can be invaluable and may even lead you down a new, more profitable path.

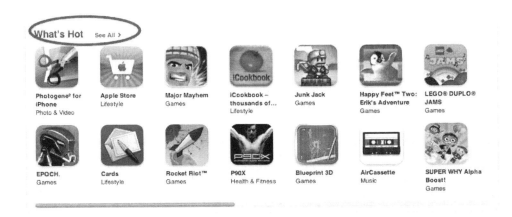

What's Hot

Use the What's Hot category to find out which apps are popular right now across various categories. On this list you'll see apps that have experienced spikes in downloads over the prior seven days. As you review this list pay attention to *why* the apps are getting more downloads. Here are some of the elements to consider:

- Has the rating improved?

- Did the developer release an update?

- Did the owner launch a new promotion?

- Was the app icon altered? (I will discuss the role that the icon plays in an app's success in a later chapter.)

• Were the app screen shots improved?

• Did the developer create and distribute a press release about the app and its functionalities?

• Was the product featured on an app review website?

Any or all of these factors can have significant impact on the number of downloads that an app gets within a given period, and its ranking on the What's Hot chart.

As you peruse the chart consider how you might be able to make the apps better – effectively "cloning" them, and then reaping your own rewards from the efforts. Keep your finger on the pulse of the What's Hot list and over time you'll pick up on patterns surrounding the most popular app styles, and you'll get some great ideas for your own products.

Bonus Resource!

 In this book we covered the Apple charts, but the same principles apply to every platform. One of the bonuses I offered you with this book was the *How To Create Apps Blueprint + Video Introduction* where I explain 25 different locations to get ideas for apps. You can get instant access to the $128 worth of bonuses by visiting the members' area.

www.howtomakemillionsfromapps.com/bookmembers

When you are looking at the App Store's top free apps make sure you assess exactly how these apps are actually making money, because they are. The best way to figure this out is by downloading the apps and either play or use them to figure out what the monetization strategy is. This will help you understand the dynamics and apply the best principles with your own apps.

After all, if you don't test these apps out yourself and interact with them how can you properly design and create apps that are also going to be popular and profitable? You would literally have to start from scratch and learn your way by trial and error –

41

something you <u>don't</u> want to do!

Shhh....Insider App Secret!

I've gotten some of the best ideas for improving my own apps by downloading and interacting with other applications on the market – most of them free. This allows me to see how other companies are marketing and promoting their products, using different buttons to promote user engagement, or employing technologies like push notification or gain involvement mechanisms. I've learned how to add thousands of dollars in revenue to my bottom line every year and you can too.

Even if you plan to offer a paid app, creating a free version can be a valuable marketing strategy. It will help you promote more downloads and entice people to test out other versions of your app.

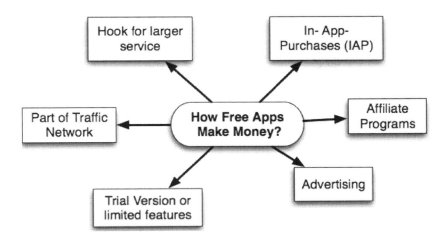

I'm sure you've downloaded a fair number of free applications to your own iPad, iPhone, Android, or Blackberry. After all, who can resist a "free" opportunity to try out something that might be fun to play, or that might make your life simpler or your workload smaller? The question that you probably ask yourself when you take advantage of these free offers is, "How in the world do these guys make any money off of these apps?"

There are a few different answers to that question. One of the ways free apps make money is through in-app purchases, which allow customers to purchase upgrades, buy new content, and acquire complementary features directly within your application.

In-app purchases are new and expanding elements within the app ecosystem. An effective way to develop your own in-app strategy is by downloading a few of the top, free apps and learning firsthand how those developers are using the innovations to make money. When you visit an app store and click on a map, for example, all of the in-app purchases (with the current prices) are listed in the app details.

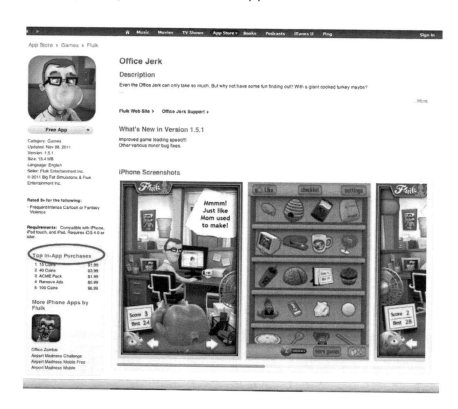

(The screenshot above from the Apple App Store highlights where you can see the top in-app purchases for this particular game.)

Jot down some notes as you review the in-app details on the top free apps. Create a reference document where you can take notes on the details that you're collecting, including exactly how much money other developers are charging for which items.

As you go through this exercise you'll see that companies change their prices and items (this is called "testing the offer," in marketing speak) regularly in order to find the sweet spot – that exact price point that attracts customers without giving the offer away for too little money.

Use the in-app purchase research to help fast track your success in the app market and to stoke revenue growth. You will be surprised that even free games are offering IAP bundles up to $99. If you create an app and you are not offering IAP's you are severely limiting your profits and app success.

In the App Success System I explain over 25 different types of In-App Purchases that you can implement into your app. So if you are thinking that IAP's don't apply to your app you are wrong. Check out the App Success System at www.AppSuccessSystem.com

Ranking and Review Sites

Locating specific information within the Apple App Store can be challenging, namely due to the way the site is laid out and organized. The good news is that there are many other websites that will make your life easier by simplifying the task of finding valuable data on other applications.

Here are some resources that you'll want to check out:

www.appannie.com

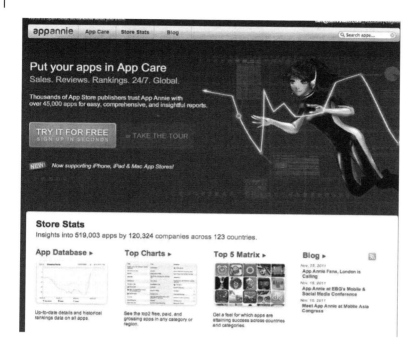

This is a great website that provides insight and analytics into the current trends within the App Store. On the site you'll find sales reviews, rankings, and worldwide rank reports. The latter is particularly useful because every country has its own app ecosystem – what's popular in one may not be popular in another.

App Annie is also great for researching new app ideas and offers these useful features:

The Top 5 Matrix

Here you'll be able to see the top five matrixes for paid, free, and top-grossing for every country that has an App Store. You will be able to change these categories based on country of interest and the specific app categories that you are assessing. Understanding the top five apps in any category you want to sell into is extremely important and App Annie gives you this information quickly and efficiently. Click on the icons you'll gain access to more detailed information about specific applications.

Idea Time...

Here is where you can start writing down your ideas. It is ok to make notes in this book in the margins or on the back of pages. You will thank me later.

✓ What ideas do you have for an app?

✓ How can you make money with this app?

✓ What features will you offer?

✓ What updates could you publish?

✓ How can you modify to create clones or new versions?

Top Charts

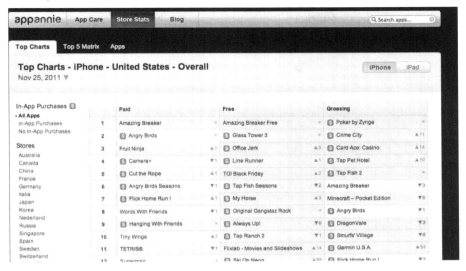

Use the Top Charts feature on App Annie to see which apps include in-app purchases and which ones do not. You can then quickly assess the app's in-app purchases and figure out how to incorporate them into your own app ideas. Be sure to explore the app descriptions to see how the in-app offers are laid out.

Shhh...Insider App Secret!

Customer ratings and reviews can reveal a lot about what people don't like about a particular app. By reading through these rants you can pick up on the flaws and gaps in the existing apps and then figure out ways to improve upon them with your own product. This spells out real opportunity: release an app with the features that users want – and that they didn't find in other offerings – and you'll see your download numbers rise exponentially.

You can read the apps reviews within the App Store, on websites like App Annie or other app review sites mentioned in this chapter. Also check out YouTube, where you can watch videos of people reviewing and rating apps. In today's information age, people speak pretty freely about what frustrates them, what they like, and what they don't. This is all you need to know to make your own apps!

More Great Idea Sources

You'll find some great app ideas in places where you probably never thought to look. Toys "R" Us (www.toysrus.com), for example, features top-selling kids' toys for various age groups. If you plan to hit the "kids and moms" market segment you'll want to check out this site for some great game ideas. Look at what's already popular with kids and moms and figure out a way to turn an existing idea into something new.

Here are some other websites that can be useful for finding out what is popular right now, and then creating apps based on those successes:

http://appdata.com/
http://www.insidemobileapps.com/
http://www.games.com/
http://www.addictinggames.com/
http://www.gametop.com/

There's no question that games are hot, hot, hot in the app space right now – and their popularity isn't expected to wane anytime soon. Unless there is a specific reason why you <u>don't</u> want to tackle this category (like if you've developed an app that will help research scientists cure a fatal disease), you'll definitely want to add one or more games to your app portfolio.

Idea Time…

Take action and start making notes about your ideas…what could you do with your app? How can you turn this into an app? How could you improve this app idea? Along with the list below start making notes and create app ideas list.

As you go over your options in this category, consider these top game styles:

Maze-Type Games:

- ✓ Rail Maze
- ✓ Bomberman
- ✓ Traffic Rush
- ✓ Mouse Maze
- ✓ Tilt Maze

Board Games

- ✓ Tic Tac Toe
- ✓ Battleship
- ✓ Chess
- ✓ Connect Four
- ✓ Stratego

Simulation Games

- ✓ SimCity
- ✓ Crimson Pirates

Action Games

- ✓ Harbor Master
- ✓ Flight Control
- ✓ Spy Mouse
- ✓ Cooking Dash
- ✓ Field Runners
- ✓ Ant Smasher
- ✓ Hard Lines

Fast track your success with App Source Codes.

Tigga Studios offers a complete source code library to get you building apps faster and cheaper.

Watch a free 40 min video where Ben explains the advantages of buying app sources codes when publishing apps.

www.BuyAppsSourceCodes.com

Tigga Studios also offers complete turn-key app portfolio where they create, design, and publish apps to your developer account, for you.

Puzzle Games

- ✓ Unblock Me
- ✓ Plants VS Zombies
- ✓ Tetris
- ✓ Bubble Shooter Pro
- ✓ Dots Premium
- ✓ Minesweeper
- ✓ Shinro Minesweeper
- ✓ Aces Traffic Pack

Word Games

- ✓ Scrabble
- ✓ Sudoku
- ✓ Bejeweled
- ✓ BookWorm

Role Playing Games

- ✓ Zenonia
- ✓ Roman Empire

Social Games *

- ✓ DragonVale
- ✓ Tap Zoo
- ✓ Tiny Pets
- ✓ Farmville
- ✓ Restaurant Story

✓ Tiny Village

From this short list of games you should be able to generate enough ideas to last a lifetime!

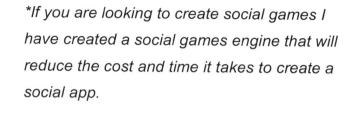

If you are looking to create social games I have created a social games engine that will reduce the cost and time it takes to create a social app.

Contact Tigga Studios and speak to our team about how we can make your social app idea a reality by using our advanced multiplatform game social app engine. I guarantee you will save time and money. *www.TiggaStudios.com*

Kick off your own game strategy by adding to the list of games that you just read through. Then, watch a few different game videos on YouTube. Write down 10 ideas within five minutes and then whittle your list down to a few viable options. Before you know it, you will be rolling out your own innovative game ideas.

Shhh...Insider App Secret!

When you are developing your own games try not to over-complicate them. Instead, come up with games that people can play anywhere, at any time, on their mobile devices. When you are starting out publish fast and cheap and move on to more expensive and complicated games. Start with apps that you can get published in 60 days or less.

Think Fun

As you've seen from this chapter, the top 25 app list is primarily comprised of games and fun utilities, which means that a focus on fun can take you a long way in the app development world (at least right now and into the foreseeable future). The ranking of the 25 top free apps is similar, although there are usually a few productivity and social networking (like Facebook) apps thrown into the mix.

 Once you've reviewed the lists one of your first thoughts will probably be: How can I take a concept that's already popular, change it around a bit, and create a new design that's 100 percent unique? If the answer doesn't hit you immediately, go back to the list (maybe the top 50 this time) and look at the popular apps that are actually clones of the leading apps. Maybe they have different character styles and maybe the game play has been altered, but at their core these clones are clearly based on existing products.

Just to reiterate: there's no need to reinvent the wheel, particularly when you're developing your first few apps. Just look at what's already generating a healthy revenue stream and figure out a way to make it better.

There are a lot of developers out there who are tightly focused on creating the next Angry Bird-style of game and that's great for them. Maybe they have deep pockets or just a lot of time and expertise at their avail. Much like the guy who bets big in Las Vegas hoping to win millions, these folks are focused on the big win. They want to hit the jackpot...or nothing.

I'm here to tell you that you can take a less aggressive approach to app development and still come out ahead financially. For example, you could create utility-based apps (such as time converters, calculators, maps, and barcode scanners – the list goes on) that people will download regularly for a fee.

The audience for utility-based apps is very large so don't limit yourself into thinking you need to create the next Words With Friends in order to be successful. What you should focus on instead is building a portfolio of apps (and not just a single program) that provides you with a stable, predictable income.

Universal Appeal

When I'm developing apps I like to come up with innovations that cater to several market niches. I also look for ideas that have broad appeal on a 24/7, 365-day basis. That way I don't have to worry about seasonally-based apps, which usually lead to seasonal income streams. That said, seasonal apps can be a great addition to your portfolio, but just don't make them your only income stream. You'll wind up with download spikes and then significant lulls when Christmas, Halloween, or Easter is over. (Cover all of the holidays and seasons, however, and the effort may pay off as you experience year-round download spikes!)

Another way to diversify your app portfolio is to look at what's going on in different countries and in offline marketplaces (like your local Toys "R" Us store). Think about how you can bring the popular offline concepts into a virtual application.

Consider the fact that children, teens, and adults are all interested in board games, card games, and other diversions that they can play during their downtimes. My dad plays solitaire on his mobile phone and competes with his wife to obtain the highest score. Think about the people around you and how they're using – or how they'd like to use – apps to create enjoyment in their lives. Chances are very good that there's a whole audience of potential customers out there that feel the same way.

In the next chapter we'll get down to business and start developing a scope document for your first app. If you're ready to get started, just turn the page...

Key Points to Remember from Chapter Two

- ✓ Apps don't have to be original; they can be better versions of what's already out there.
- ✓ Free apps make money through in-app purchases, upgrades, and other monetization mechanisms.
- ✓ Reviewing the app charts regularly will give you some great ideas of what's out there, and where your own app ideas will fit into the bigger picture.
- ✓ Games are a particularly good category to target when creating your first few apps.

Chapter Three:

Defining Your Scope Document

A scope document outlines the functionality and design elements of your application. This document will serve as the cornerstone for the development process and will help you determine how cost effectively and quickly your application can be built.

The scope document should not be complicated, complex, or difficult to understand. Much like a business plan – which spells out how a company will operate and make money in its industry by targeting specific marketers – the scope document simply defines and guides your app development project.

When creating your scope document you'll set realistic budgets and lay out the framework for your app.

Key Elements of a Scope Document

There are some specific sections you will want to include in your scope document. These elements will help you completely define your application and determine its viability. (Some developers refer to the contents of the scope document as the "wireframe document" because it outlines how every action within the application is connected.)

The more clearly you define how your application works for your developers and designers, the faster and more cost-effectively they will be able to produce your application. Being overly vague at this stage of the game may result in thousands of dollars in added costs and long development time frames – all due to poor communication. I've seen this happen on several occasions and it's something you'll want to avoid at all costs.

Here are some of the main sections to include in your scope document:

1. Objective
2. App functionality
    a. Core functionality
    b. Additional or optional functionality
3. Design layout mock
    a. Design references
    b. Menu/ tab layout
    c. App wireframe

4. App walk-through

5. In-App Purchase

6. Reference applications or functionality

As you begin to create your own document, be sure to clearly define your application and to keep things simple. One of the fastest ways to do this is with Keynote, PowerPoint, or a simple Word or Pages document. This will help you keep your thoughts, research, and information organized and will make the document easy to share with others.

Shhh…Insider App Secret!

Your scope document doesn't have to be complicated, but it does need to clearly state what you're trying to achieve and the functionality that you want from within your app. This will help prevent what is called "scope creep," which we will discuss in a later chapter.

Here's a closer look at each element that will go into your scope document, and an explanation of each:

Objective: This is the mission statement or purpose statement of your application. Clearly define the objective in as few words as possible.

App functionality: Here's where you'll list all of the functionality that you want from within your application. Be sure to include what the app will do, how will it do it, what happens when it's done, and what services it integrates with.

Core functionality: This area will spell out the application's functionalities that will be released in Stage I. You'll outline the vital framework that will make your app successful and also include information like: How will I get feedback from users? How will people rate and comment on the app? How will I collect their email addresses (for follow up and future marketing)? How will my app make money? These are very important considerations that you'll want to think out carefully and insert into this section of your scope document.

Additional or optional functionality: You may or may not want to address this section during Stage I, but it will definitely come into play during Stage II and Stage III. That's because you'll be using user feedback and other resources to hone your app and make it even more relevant and attractive to your target audience. You want developers to be *thinking ahead* to these additional and/or optional functionalities. In some cases, for example, your developers may tell you that due to the simplicity of certain functionalities, they can be easily included in Stage I.

This will help you get ahead of the game and allow you to think even further advance in terms of adding new functions and capabilities to your program. You can keep your finger on the pulse of future updates and release options, and market and promote your app in a way that encourages more and more downloads. This is the Holy Grail and it should be what you're shooting for as you develop your app portfolio.

Design layout mock: This is where you can start to visualize your app and how it will look on a user's mobile or tablet screen. You'll lay out the look and feel of the application screen-by-screen and step-by-step. Take the time to think about exactly how you want your application laid out and designed. Also consider how you can simplify the design – a strategy that you'll want to use throughout the application development process.

When developing this aspect of your scope document it's a good idea to study some of the top grossing applications (outlined in the last chapter) to see how simple and Zen-like these apps are. Interestingly enough, in many cases the simplest apps take more thought and planning that the complicated, memory-hogging programs. Put some thought into this step and work closely with your graphic designer, who will likely complete numerous revisions before coming up with a final product.

Key changes that will take place during this stage include alterations to the app's menu and changes to the button shapes, positions, and colors. Users will see and focus on these elements first, so be sure to put some thought into how you want them to look. Test out different versions and work with your developer to ensure a streamlined, user-friendly experience for the folks who download your app.

You'll find plenty of simple, drag-and-drop software solutions that will help you create design mocks even if you are not a professional designer. Here are some of those solutions that you can test out:

Note that these options are not listed in any order or

preference. You can assess which tools will be best for your situation:

http://mockapp.com

http://www.appcooker.com/

http://www.groosoft.com/

http://www.endloop.ca/imockups/

Shhh…Insider App Secret!

If you want to keep things very simple you can use Keynote or PowerPoint by downloading app icon templates. You insert the icons as images into your presentation and manipulate them to produce the design mocks. Remember keep it simple, use Screenflow or Camtasia to record yourself speaking about the app and explaining it. Then you have something you can share with graphic designers, coders or programmers.

Here are a few good user interface template resources that you'll want to check out when developing your own screen-by-screen app shots:

1) At the link below you'll find an article that provides you with 50 free user interface templates you can use for building your apps.

Designers always need some basic user interface elements to create a model of user interface either of a website or software. For that, they need wire framing and UI design kits which help them mock-up the user interface. Read more:

http://www.smashingapps.com/2011/02/02/50-free-web-ui- mobile-ui-wireframe-kits-and-source-files-for-designers.html

2) Here's another good resource to explore.

Here are some great UI mockup resources that you can use when designing your app ideas.

http://blog.metaspark.com/2009/02/fireworks-toolkit-for- creating-iphone-ui-mockups/

3) And a final resource that you'll want to check out.

So you have a killer idea for an iPhone app, but when you describe it to people they just don't get it. Maybe you have a client that is a visual thinker and needs you to draw it out for him. That's when wireframes, mockups and stencils can be your saving grace. Use this resource to create app prototypes:

http://iphoneized.com/2009/11/21-prototyping-mockup- wireframing-tools-iphone-app-development/

Here's a final note for those of you who like to draw and create your ideas the "old fashioned" way, by hand. I've created a PDF file that you can download and then use to outline your ideas by hand. You'll find the PDF at this link:

http://howtomakemillionswithapps.com/?p=305

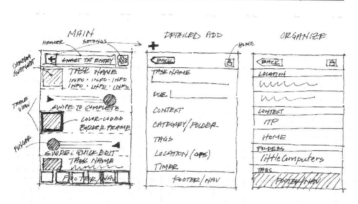

Design references: In this section of the scope document you get to use your research and provide reference applications or design resources to your coders and designers. These materials will visually represent exactly what you want your app to look like.

Completing this step may be as simple as providing links to other apps in the App Store. Include all elements from websites that you like. You may be providing references to videos on YouTube and/or other gaming sources. At the end of the day the more information you can provide that clearly defines the style and design elements you want from in your application, the easier the development process is going to be (and the happier you will be with the ultimate outcome!).

Menu/ tab layout: Menus are very important because your users will rely on them to help them navigate through the application and its various functionalities. Think about how you want your menu laid out, how you can simplify your menu titles, and what the submenus will be. Keep user functionality in mind as you go through this process, and strive to keep things as clear and simple as possible.

App wireframe: This is the fun part of the scope document. It's where you will connect all of the dots from within your application and think about how the app is going to function once someone downloads it and starts playing with it. In some cases you can skip this step. If, for example, your app is simple enough, then your developer will be able to work out this aspect of the scope document. A word of warning if you do choose to take this route: it's always best to clearly define the app wireframe and its associated steps. This will help you understand exactly what you're paying a developer and/or coder to produce for you. You don't want any unnecessary surprises to creep up at the last minute.

As you can see, the scope document is a fairly comprehensive piece of work that provides clear guidance for the developers who will bring your app to life. The document itself needn't be complicated, but it should be concise and detailed enough to provide solid guidance and get you to your end goal as quickly and affordably as possible!

Some of my best apps have been built from simple documents that I've created in PowerPoint or Keynote. I clearly defined the objectives and the functionality of the application in the documents. By walking through this process I was able to determine all of the elements of the application and myriad other details that came in handy when I was working with my developer.

As you learned in this chapter, you certainly don't have to start from scratch or go it alone when creating the initial plans for your app. There are many different software programs that you can use to create a visual mock design of your app. Taking the time to use these tools will help your developers and designers develop your app, and it will give you solid insights into what you can expect from the final product.

When designing apps I stick to one cardinal rule: the design must be simple enough for a 5-year-old child to use. Granted, these youngsters are probably more tech-savvy than many adults are right now, but the bottom line is this: if a kid can't use your app, it's not going to sell.

People tend to go in the other direction when developing apps, assuming that the more complicated the programs are, the more enticing they will be to potential users. This is not the case. In fact, going too complex is a fatal mistake that many app owners make. Here are a few areas where they go wrong:

- ✓ They don't take the time to create quality graphics that visually explain how to use the application.
- ✓ They overwhelm the user with choices, thus paralyzing the customer and virtually ensuring that he or she never gets interested in the application.
- ✓ They don't clearly outline the options.
- ✓ They provide more than three actions to take at any one time.

We live in a society where people want extremely simple solutions to very complex problems. They want to lose weight, make more money, have fun, and be happy. App developers who can tap into these and other desires and provide simple ways to achieve some aspect of these goals will come out the winners. The developers that make lives even more complicated with complex, unintelligible directions, menus, and interfaces, will quickly find themselves back at their drawing boards.

You Can Do It Yourself

The DIY approach to app development isn't as hard as it looks, particularly if you already have some programming and/or software development experience. This isn't something you'll want to venture into if you're a newbie who is trying to develop numerous apps for a portfolio in a short amount of time, but it can be the right choice for some people. Not only will you learn the ropes of app development, but you'll also save a significant amount of money and retain 100 percent control over your project.

There are many books and web resources that you can reference if you want to learn how to develop apps from scratch. If you choose this route you'll also have a few resources at your avail. iPhone and iPod Touch DIY app developers like AppMakr and MyAppBuilder both allow users to create their own programs and GENWI released its first iPad-specific app-making tool in 2011. Here's how the company defines its product:

GENWI's iPad app creation features will inspire you to build compelling iPad apps. The new iPad solution is fully customizable and offers a tailor-made, branded experience for publishers. The unique flexible client architecture, adding new content and updates to apps in real time, helps publishers to create visually stunning and live updated media apps. Optimized templates and themes are offered to help jump-start the design process.

> CSS is also offered as an advanced option, allowing publishers to create almost any user experience or design imaginable. Media publishers can rapidly transform a print magazine into a visually stunning and custom branded tablet app. The utility costs about $499-per-month, for which GENWI processes the publishing and offers instant distribution and real-time updates pulled from the data sources.

New tools are coming out every day, and are aimed at app owners who – much like individuals who want to skirt web developers and use templates to create their own websites – like the DIY approach. There are pros and cons to using this approach so explore your options carefully before deciding on a good solution.

Another great solution is the free app building tool from conduit.com. This simple online tool allows you to develop, deploy and promote mobile apps on Apple IOS, Android, Windows, Blackberry and Bada for free. It is a great solution for local businesses, bands, or web based media apps.

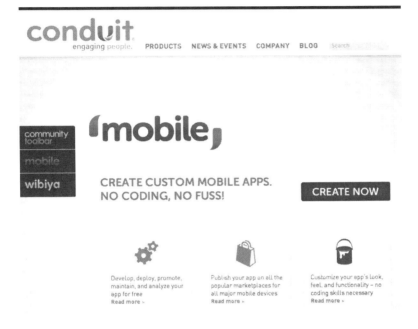

Remember: if you don't like the results of your first attempt, you can always use a designer and developer to improve on what you've created (for your product's Stage II) and then move forward with the rest of your ideas.

Shhh…Insider App Secret!

I have created my own app builder which is a free resource. You can create and publish apps on various platforms. This tool was developed by marketers for marketers. So if you want a simple tool to build apps this may be exactly what you need.

www.howtomakemillionswithapps.com/appbuilder

Tricks That Make Development Easier

In the final section of this chapter I'd like to focus on a few key tips that will make the app development process easier for you. Since app development is fairly "new" by comparison (namely since apps didn't hit the mainstream until the iPhone made its debut a few years ago), the information swirling around the industry tends to be muddled and a bit murky at best.

I'm here to help. I've compiled the following laundry list of app tips that you should keep in mind when creating your own fun and useful apps. Here's what I came up with:

1. **Focus on continuous improvement:** Development doesn't end with Stage I. Look carefully at how your app can be improved, listen to user feedback, and focus on improving the quality and functionality of your app on a regular basis.

2. **Aim for the highest standards of quality**. Make sure your apps meet all of the needs and requirements of your users. If they don't, it's time to revisit the development process and improve your offering.

3. **Focus on the user experience:** Make your mobile app easy to use. Don't confuse the user or make him jump through hoops to get to the core of your app. Put yourself in his shoes: would you want to spend hours trying to learn how to use a new app? Of course not.

4. **Don't overlook mobile security.** Make sure your developer has sorted out and addressed all of the underlying security issues <u>before</u> your app goes live.

5. **Don't try too hard.** Unlike bloated software programs that weigh down even the most memory-intensive computer systems, apps are light and fun. They address one specific issue or deliver one particularly fun experience. Don't try too hard – just do it!

6. **Test, test, test...and then test again.** Don't take any shortcuts here. Test your mobile app to make sure that it's bug-free and that the coding works like it's supposed to. Don't release a half-baked app. Instead, send it back to the developer for more work and honing.

7. **Make the app applicable across many devices.** Screen resolution, screen size, font size, colors, and contrast differ across the various devices currently in use. They can wreak havoc on even the most universally developed apps. Put simply: not everyone has an iPhone or Droid, so be sure to test your app on as many devices as possible before going live. One way to ensure that the app is viewable and useable across many different devices is to use high-contrast color schemes and widgets that are differentiated with blocks of solid color (as opposed to shaded boxes or outlines).

8. **Watch your fonts.** Most mobile phone fonts are too small to read without adjustment. This correlates with the small screen size and is something to bear in mind when developing your app. The trick is to make the fonts as large as possible without detracting from the visual content. Doing this will greatly increase the odds that the folks who download your app will actually use it.

9. **He who opts for simplicity always wins.** You've heard this before in this book and I'll say it again here: keep your app simple. Despite popular belief, there is no direct correlation between the number of features in an app and the number of downloads it gets. In fact, some of the simplest apps are the most popular and consistently rank on the top 10 lists.

10. **Make them want more.** You want to whet your users' appetites for your app. Make them <u>want</u> to upgrade to the full, paid version. Make them <u>want</u> to register. Make them feel like they are missing out on some really great stuff if they <u>don't</u> take these steps. With so many apps on the market your job is to stand out from the clutter and make users want more from your app – and more apps from you.

11. **Focus on performance.** No one has the time or patience to sit around and wait for apps to load. Ensure that the load times for your app are as short as possible, and that the transitions within the app are also brisk.

12. **Document your progress.** This is a development tip that you won't want to ignore: document everything related to the app's development and retain copies of those documents. If you decide to change developers or make significant changes to your app's architecture you'll have the reference materials at your fingertips to be able to answer the question, "What did the last guy do?" This will save you time and money, and it will ensure that enhancements and upgrades take just a few days to implement, not months. Also document your daily app stats, this will help you track changes that you make to your apps and how that effects your revenues, downloads, time within your app and much more. This information will help you make informed choices about how to market and

promote you apps.

In the next chapter I'll show you how to assemble a development team and get your first app off of the drawing board and into the creation stage.

Key Points to Remember from Chapter Three

- ✓ Your scope document needn't be complex, but it does need to include several key elements.
- ✓ You can build an app yourself using one of several template/software applications available on the market.
- ✓ Keeping your app simple is one of the basic development tenets that you won't want to ignore.
- ✓ Performance, font size, colors, and myriad other graphical elements can make or break an app, so pay attention to these details.

Chapter Four:

Assembling a Development Team

Now it's time to learn how to assemble a great development team. This is a particularly important chapter since your team will serve as the backbone for your entire project. The ideas and visions may come from you, but these folks will be the people who bring your aspirations to life.

If you've ever hired people before as part of your job, or selected third-party providers to help out on specific projects, you'll be able to apply many of the same selection principles when you're putting a development team together.

At the most basic level you want to select folks that will work well together on a team and that possess the right amount of expertise to be able to develop your app without having to jump through a lot of hoops to get there (read: hoops = time = money). Any learning curves should be short in the interest of keeping development time to a minimum and quality at the most optimal level.

What You Need to Get Started

A great way to get started is to simply borrow a page from the 300-pound app gorilla Apple, which offers the following advice when putting together a team for in-house app development:

> As with any project, you'll want to assemble a team of contributors who each share a stake in the success and outcome of your app project. Some participants may be your internal customers, and others will be tasked with owning specific parts of the development process itself.

Ultimately, you want to align the team roles and responsibilities with the project timeline and milestones discussed in the prior step. For example, because design is a central element of any development project, you'll want to make sure you have a design team (or resources to match). Different groups may have different points of participation and interest in the outcome, so it's important to document those roles so that everyone can stay abreast of responsibilities along the way.

In your case you'll likely serve as the project owner and leader, the latter of which tracks schedules, timelines, and the overall scope of the work. As your app business expands you may want to hire someone to help you with these tasks, or you may prefer to keep them close to the vest. It's up to you and it will largely depend on how much time you have at your avail and the number of projects that are on your plate at any given time.

Here are a few other roles that you'll either handle on your own or outsource to a third party or an employee:

- ✓ User Experience Architect: Responsible for framework of user interaction model and user process flow/journey.
- ✓ Technical Architect: Responsible for infrastructure, security, and data access models.
- ✓ User Interface Designer: Responsible for app visual design, graphics, and identity
- ✓ Developer: Responsible for overall technical architecture and coding

If you don't have sufficient in-house resources to cover these various tasks, Apple suggests outsourcing all or part of the development work. Outsourced developers can also present you with a portfolio of their work that could spark new ideas. Of course, to be successful, the outsourced team needs a thorough understanding of your project - everything you've determined during the planning process - and regular interaction with you and your in-house team.

Discuss your needs and make sure they understand what your objectives are. Review the application definition statement and carefully review your project details. And be sure right from the start that you've established clear, two-way communication and a process for keeping in touch.

Shhh....Insider App Secret!

Do not give up a percentage or ownership of your app if you do not have to. Instead, pay upfront for work completed. In the long run it will become much cheaper. It is not expensive to get your apps created, so just pay for it. You will thank me later...

Dealing with Developers

App development is a hot job opportunity for programmers who are interested in this kind of work. Unfortunately, there aren't always enough of these IT-types to go around, so you may have to put some elbow grease into your search. According to the Wall

Street Journal, for example, the number of mobile development jobs offered on Elance.com, a freelancer website, doubled between the first quarters of 2010 and in 2011; the job opportunities grew at a pace that was twice as fast as growth on the entire Elance.com site as a whole.

When selecting an app developer be sure to:

- ✓ Meet multiple vendors.
- ✓ Review existing work, including apps on the App Store; note app ranking and user comments.
- ✓ Evaluate skills and capabilities; for example, is all coding done in-house?
- ✓ Ask for references.
- ✓ Disregard the one-size-fits-all ethic or generic multiplatform approach.
- ✓ Focus on UI design, high-quality art, and the app "journey."
- ✓ Discuss maintenance and life cycle of app beyond version 1.0.
- ✓ Ask about IT infrastructure experience.

Source: Apple In-House App Accelerator Guide

Before approaching anyone about your project, sharing your idea, or requesting a quote, be sure that you have an idea of exactly what you expect from this person. This will help tremendously when it comes time to convey your ideas and ensure that your requests are executed properly (refer to your scope document for a lot of this information). If you have taken the time to complete your scope document this should be clear to you and to them by now.

Shhh....Insider App Secret!

Depending on the sensitivity of the information you'll be sharing you may also want to ask the developer to sign an NDA (non-disclosure agreement) that will prohibit that person from sharing any information related to your work with any other parties. As part of the bonuses with this book you have access to a NDA, so log into the members' area now so you can start using it.

Another major consideration will be whether the developer specializes in just one platform (iPad, iPhone, Android, etc.) or if he or she can develop cross-platform products. This may not be a huge concern for Stage I of your very first app, but it won't take long for you to realize that the wider the breadth of your product line, the more income you'll be able to generate. Keep this in mind as you expand past your first app.

Don't forget to consider your budget. Getting a custom app developed by professionals can cost $10,000 and up. A quick search for professionals on a site like Elance or oDesk might turn up cheaper options (see the section in this chapter on "Where to Find Them"), but be sure to balance experience and expertise with cost, and never shop solely on price.

Coders are basically computer programmers. They design, write, test, debut, and maintain the source code for computer programs – or computer applications in this case. The code is written in one or more programming languages and basically lays out which specific operations result in which behaviors.

You can apply many of the steps outlined in the previous section – and those that you'll find later on in this chapter – when selecting a good coder to work with.

If you want to do your own coding, and if you're not experienced in this area, you can manage at least a part of the task with an app like FieldTest (http://fieldtestapp.com), a browser-based tool that helps turn your ideas for mobile applications and websites into interactive prototypes.

Just remember that coders are very focused on the coding platform and sometimes do not see the bigger picture or understand marketing. It's your job to provide clear instructions and manage the project through to completion. If you do not provide clear instruction, or skip the scope document development step, you will pay for it during the design and development stage.

Locating Good Team Members

Good team members may exist in the company you currently work for, or you may be able to connect with a few through social networking sites like Facebook, Twitter, and LinkedIn (search the latter for app developers and see what you come up with). College computer science and programming interns from your local schools may also be able to help.

Freelance sites abound online and specialize in connecting outsourced providers with paying clients. Here are a few to check out:

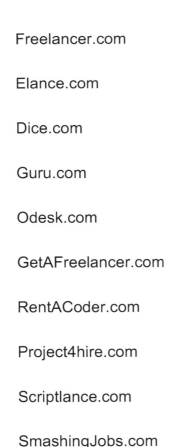

Freelancer.com

Elance.com

Dice.com

Guru.com

Odesk.com

GetAFreelancer.com

RentACoder.com

Project4hire.com

Scriptlance.com

SmashingJobs.com

SimplyHired.com

On most of these sites you will register as an "employer" and begin posting jobs online. "Providers" will answer the call by bidding on your projects. You'll find a good selection of potential providers on the sites listed above, all of which are either dedicated to IT projects and/or have a substantial presence in this area.

Shhh....Insider App Secret!

When you are looking for providers make sure you, 1. Check their past work; 2. Never pay upfront in full always pay on a milestone basis; 3. Trust your gut instinct; 4. Have  multiple conversations with them; 5. Remember that you are the boss.

Thinking Locally

Another way to find good app developers is by making connections in your local community. Many IT professionals attend meetups, conferences, and other networking events. Here's what one Boston blogger had to say about finding good app developers in his community:

"One of the best ways to connect with local developers is by meeting them directly at some of the area's regularly scheduled Meetups and events. Boston's got one of the

largest and most active mobile communities in the world, and there are typically at least a few great events, Meetups, or conferences scheduled each month to choose from. Find a topic that interests you and register in less than a minute online. Most are more casual than you might expect (beer is often available) and give people an opportunity to network, discuss ideas, and announce any job openings or projects. The best developers are typically found via referrals, so even if you don't find someone to build your application, you'll definitely talk to people who can give you suggestions or perhaps even connect you with the right people."

Here are a few suggestions for finding these events and venues:

- Meetup.com — There are tons of Meetups to choose from each month covering a variety of mobile topics and interests.
- Eventbrite.com — Eventbrite's a great online resource to discover local mobile events, conferences, and classes. Simply search for a topic such as "mobile" or "iPhone" in your area to discover upcoming events by a variety of great organizations.
- iPhone Developers Roundtable Message Board – Check out the Job Openings message board for local Meetup communities of mobile enthusiasts and developers. A job posted here will be seen by some of the best and brightest around.
- Twitter, Facebook, & LinkedIn – Tap your friends, family, and colleagues on Twitter, Facebook, LinkedIn,

and other networks for people they may know. Again, the best talent is usually discovered via referrals, so don't forget to explore your online social circles for any suggestions.

Source: Jonathon Kardos, How to Find a Mobile App Developer in Boston

As you've read here, there are dozens of places to find good developers, coders, project managers, and other professionals who can help you take your idea from concept to completion. Remember to keep budget in mind – but don't make it your only priority – when selecting the right professionals to work with.

If you want more information on how to find good people check out Benjamin's training course. He has spent over $500,000 outsourcing since 2000. **Fast track your success visit** <u>**www.AppSuccessSystem.com**</u>

Hiring & Firing

I could write an entire book on how to hire, test, and fire app developers, but there are plenty of human resource management books already available on the marketplace. The bottom line is that you'll want to choose carefully when deciding on an app developer to work with. Test him or her out on a small portion of your project first. If it doesn't work out, try someone else.

Like anything in life, finding the right partner to help advance your cause can be frustrating. Keep your eyes open to the challenges and be patient, but not to the point where you are throwing money and time down the drain. If things aren't progressing as planned, ask questions. If the questions go unanswered – or if you're not satisfied with the answers that you're getting – move on to another provider.

Shhh....Insider App Secret!

If your project is nearing completion and at least 90 percent satisfactory then you might want to hold off on firing the provider until the current project is done. Bringing someone new onboard could set you back, both financially and time-wise.

Here are a few good tips to use when hiring app developers:

- ✓ Look through the developer's portfolio and work experience.
- ✓ Ask for recommendations from previous clients.
- ✓ Get registered as a developer with one or more sites (see next chapter on how to do this).
- ✓ Use a confidentiality agreement or an NDA.
- ✓ Know your app requirements and details <u>before</u> your first conversation with the provider.
- ✓ Map out your app requirements clearly to help the developer understand your goals.

✓ Draw up a budget so that you can be ready to discuss pricing details on the spot.

So you have the lowdown on what it takes to put together a solid development team. Now we'll take a look at the basic steps you'll need to take to get your app published. If you're ready to learn more, flip on over to the next chapter.

Key Points to Remember from Chapter Four

✓ Your development team will play an important role in your app's success.
✓ Consider online and local sources when seeking providers.
✓ Have a plan in mind before you start your talent search.
✓ Be ready to discuss budget during your first conversation with the developer.

Chapter Five:
Get Your App Published

Getting your app published is probably one of the most exciting aspects of this whole process. This is where the idea comes to light. Everything that just a few months or years ago was floating around in your head is now out in the open and ready for all to see, use, and enjoy.

Hopefully by now any bugs and flaws will be worked out of the application and it will be ready for its big debut. If not, be sure to fix these issues before going live. You don't want a handful of unhappy customers to spread the word about your half-baked app. You want them to rave about it!

In this chapter we'll take a quick look at how to get set up as a developer on the primary platforms (the same process is used across most of the platforms, so once you've mastered one you'll be able to tackle them all). We'll also discuss analytics, tracking, and ad networks – all of which are important "after market" steps that you'll want to incorporate into your business plan.

Setting up your developer accounts

First let's look at Apple, since there's a pretty good chance that this going to be your first stop. As you can probably guess, this company has done a pretty good job of making the registration process user friendly and simple to work through. After all, that's what Mac is all about, right? Here's what you'll see on your first visit to the developer site:

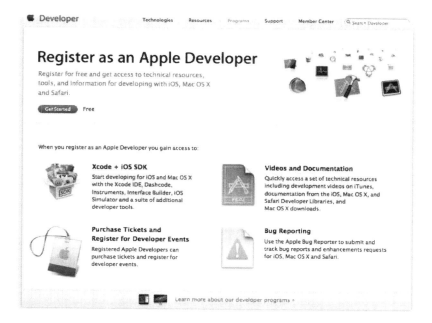

Here's a quick snapshot of the process:

Register as an Apple Developer: Register for free and get access to technical resources, tools, and information for developing with iOS, Mac OS X and Safari.

Create an Apple ID: If you have not registered as an Apple developer or do not have an iTunes, Apple Online Store or MobileMe account, you will need to create an Apple ID.

Use an existing Apple ID: If you have already registered as an Apple developer or have an iTunes, Apple Online Store or MobileMe account, you can use your existing Apple ID to sign in. *(Note: If you intend to enroll in a paid Developer Program for business purposes, you may prefer to create a new Apple ID that is dedicated to your business transactions and used for accounting purposes with Apple.)*

Shhh....Insider App Secret!

If you want to sell your app developer account and your app portfolio at some point in time in the future you should register as a company now. Speak with your accountant about the tax implications of generating income  under your own name if you setup a personal account. Selling a company that owns the developer account is easier than selling a personal developer account. This applies to app publishing platforms.

Once you get through the Apple ID setup you'll be asked to fill out and/or review the following (in this order):

- Personal Profile
- Professional Profile
- Legal Agreement
- Email Verification

When all these steps are completed you'll be set up and ready to get started.

The Android Marketplace uses a similar setup process (only you'll use your Google ID and password instead of your iTunes information).

Here's what you'll see when you visit the developer's page for the first time:

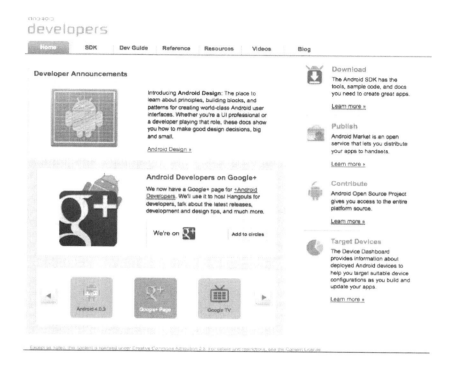

And here's the registration page that will pop up once you create a new or enter an existing Google ID:

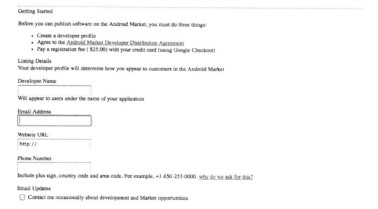

In addition to the basic registration process you'll also find some valuable information on app publishing, such as:

Any application that you publish through Android Market can use the Android Market Licensing Service. The service uses no dedicated framework APIs, so you can add licensing to any application that uses a minimum API Level of 3 or higher.

Android Market In-App Billing is an Android Market service that lets you sell digital content in your applications. You can use the service to sell a wide range of content, including downloadable content such as media files or photos, and virtual content such as game levels. When you use Android Market's in-app billing service to sell an item, Android Market handles all billing details so your application never has to directly process any financial transactions.

Android Market uses the same checkout service that is used for application purchases, so your users experience a consistent and familiar purchase flow. Also, the transaction fee for in-app purchases is the same as the transaction fee for application purchases (30%).

Publishing Apps on Android Market

Publishing your application on Android Market is a simple process that involves three basic tasks (see figure 1):

- Creating various graphical assets that accompany your app on Android Market.
- Using the Android Market Developer Console to configure publishing options, specify listing details, and upload your app and graphical assets to Android Market.
- Reviewing your publishing settings and changing the release status of your app from Unpublished to Published.

Figure 1. To publish apps on Android Market you must first prepare your app for release and then perform three simple tasks.

The last developer account we'll look at is the Amazon Appstore. With the release of the Kindle Fire in late-2011 this app store "fired up," so to speak, and is another good platform to consider when developing apps. Here's the developer intro page:

The Amazon Appstore Developer Program enables mobile application developers to sell their apps on Amazon.com. By joining the program, you can market your apps to tens of millions of Amazon customers using Amazon's proven marketing features and manage your apps using convenient self-service account management tools.

The Amazon Appstore is a new category on Amazon.com. Customers are able to shop for apps both from their PCs and mobile devices. Amazon markets your apps using proven ecommerce and marketing features like search and search refinement, browse, and app recommendations based on customers' past purchases.

The Amazon Appstore currently supports the Android operating system and works on Android devices running Android OS 1.6 and higher. Amazon pays developers 70% of the sale price of the app or 20% of the list price, whichever is greater.

To sign up you'll have to register first and then pay a $99 annual developer program fee that covers the application processing and account management for the Amazon Appstore Developer Program. (When this book went to press Amazon was still waiving the program fee for a developer's first year of the program).

You'll need to use an Amazon.com account to manage your apps in the Amazon Appstore Developer Portal. The company recommends that you create a new Amazon.com account for the Amazon Appstore Developer Program (a different account than you use for personal shopping on Amazon.com), although you may use any Amazon.com account you like.

So there you have the details on how to set up on several different developer accounts. Now we'll take a look at how to set up analytics and track those accounts.

Setting Up Analytics and Tracking Accounts

Just like website owners track the traffic and productivity of their online storefronts using analytics, you'll want to use a similar approach to track the progress and effectiveness of your app. Doing this will not only let you see how things are going, but it will also help you produce even better results by tweaking and adjusting your strategy based on the usage analytics that you've gathered.

Shhh....Insider App Secret!

You shouldn't rely solely on qualitative feedback from blogs, Facebook, and other social networking sites as a way to track your mobile app's success. Reviews aren't always the best measures either. Use the information from this chapter to set up actual analytics and tracking accounts to build and market your successful app.

Analytics are particularly effective for a couple of reasons. First, they help you enhance your application's features and usability quotient. Having the metrics at your fingertips allows you to make quick, important decisions that could have a significant impact on your revenues and success. Key metrics to explore include your app's most navigated features (where are people going when they start using your app?), how long users engage, and where the highest number of errors are generated.

Metrics also allow you to quickly figure out how many downloads are taking place within a certain amount of time, where users are geographically located, how quickly they upgrade to new versions of the app, and how your app performs when compared to other offerings on the market.

Three of the analytics programs that you'll want to check out are: Google Analytics for Android, Flurry, and Localytics. All three use a simple code that's inserted into your app's internal code and in the areas that require monitoring. The data is collected and stored on the user's smartphone, which then sends the information to the analytics software provider.

There is no impact on the app's performance due to incorporation of analytics. Further, the data streamed to the server is immediately averaged, so no one incident can be tracked in isolation. This is important for the privacy of the users.

To get set up to use an analytics and tracking account, you'll take the following steps (they are pretty much universal across all of the analytics programs):

- ✓ Sign up, create an application and pick a category (games, social, tools, business, etc.).
- ✓ Obtain a unique application key (API key) for each mobile app.
- ✓ Download the JAR file, which is then added to the application's CLASSPATH. (Your developer will handle this for you.)
- ✓ Configure the app's XML file to grant permission to collect the analytics for your app.
- ✓ The Analytics data can then be extracted using APIs or by viewing the reports online on the provider's website.

Because it's free, the Google Analytics for Mobile Apps SDKs is one of the more popular options for Android apps. It provides an interface for tracking activity within mobile apps and reporting that activity to Google Analytics. For example, you can use this SDK to calculate visits, session length, bounce rate and unique visitors.

Google Analytics for Mobile App Tracking

Here are some details from Google's site about the use of its analytics tool for mobile app tracking:

This SDK uses a tracking model that is designed to track visitors to traditional websites and interaction with widgets in traditional web pages. Use the mobile tracking SDK to track your phone applications with the following analytics interaction types:

Pageview Tracking: A pageview is a standard means to measure traffic volume to a traditional website. Because mobile apps don't contain HTML pages, you must decide when (and how often) to trigger a pageview request. Also, since pageview requests are designed to report on directory structures, you should provide descriptive names for the requests to take advantage of page path naming in the Content reports in Analytics. The names you choose will be populated in your Analytics reports as page paths, even though they are not actually HTML pages, but you can use this to your advantage by structuring paths to provide additional groupings for your calls.

Event Tracking: In Analytics, events are designed to track

user interaction to web page elements distinctly from pageview requests. You can use the Event Tracking feature of Google Analytics to make additional calls that will be reported in the Event Tracking section of the Analytics report interface. Events are grouped using categories and may also use per-event labels, which provides flexibility in reporting. For example, a multimedia app could have play/stop/pause actions for its video category and assign a label for each video name. The Google Analytics reports would then aggregate events for all events tagged with the video category.

Ecommerce Tracking: Use the Ecommerce tracking feature to track shopping cart transactions and in-app purchases. To track a transaction, use the Transaction class to represent the overall purchase information as well as the Item class to represent each product in the shopping basket. Once collected, the data can then be viewed in the Ecommerce reporting section of the Google Analytics interface.

Custom Variables: Custom variables are name-value pair tags that you can insert in your tracking code in order to refine Google Analytics tracking.

To integrate Google Analytics' tracking capabilities with your Android app, you will need:

- Android developer SDK (available for Windows, Mac OS

X, and Linux)

- Google Analytics for Mobile Apps Android SDK

Before you begin using the SDK, you must first create a free account at www.google.com/analytics and create a new web property in that account using a fake but descriptive website URL (e.g. http://mymobileapp.mywebsite.com). Once you create the property, write down or keep a copy of the web property ID that is generated for the newly-created property.

Here's what your Google Analytics dashboard will look like once you are set up:

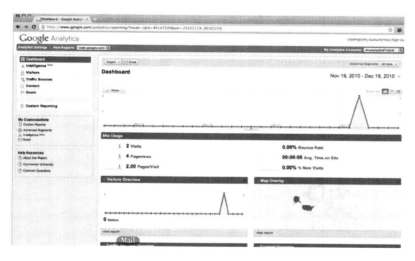

A Web property ID is also known as the UA number of your tracking code and looks like UA-xxxxx-yy, where the x's and y's indicate the unique numbers for your profile. You must indicate the web property ID you'd like to use when instantiating the tracking object.

You must indicate to your users, either in the application itself or in your terms of service, that you reserve the right to anonymously track and report a user's activity inside of your app. Your use of the Google Analytics SDK is additionally governed by the Google Analytics Terms of Service, which you must agree to when signing up for an account.

Getting your analytics and tracking accounts set up and in use will take some time and some work on the part of your developer/coder, but the payoff will be significant; trust me! You don't want to shoot from the hip online and hope that people respond well to your app. By arming yourself with the numbers on a 24/7 basis you'll be able to make adjustments and tweaks necessary to ensure the best possible success for your app business.

Setting Up Ad Networks

Global research firm Gartner expects mobile advertising spend to grow from a current $3.3 billion to $20.6 billion by 2015. That's a big chunk of change. Driving the trend is a large number of mobile phone users who are purchasing more and more apps into their lives. The more time that these folks spend on their mobile devices the more advertisers want to get their attention.

This trend puts you – the app owner – in a prime position to take advantage of a growing trend in mobile advertising. By integrating advertising into your apps in a subtle, effective manner you can greatly expand the revenue potential for your programs.

A few of the mobile advertising firms that got early footing in the industry include InMobi, Tapjoy, Millennial Media, and Jumptap. Google, which owns AdMob, and Microsoft, which developed Microsoft Mobile Advertising, are also in the game.

Mobile ads right now are generally sold on a cost-per-click (CPC) basis. The ads – which are integrated into the app's interface – direct users to a website. For example, Google provides mobile advertising solutions on a cost-per-click basis to help app developers get noticed.

Google Networks

Getting set up on the ad networks is fairly simple. Here's a quick primer on how to enable Google ads and Google certified ad networks in your applications (from the company's website):

How do I enable Google ads and ads from Google certified ad networks for my application?

Publishers can enable or disable AdSense ads for an individual app by clicking the "Manage Settings" button under their app's name in the "Sites & Apps" tab and then clicking the "App Settings" tab. Please note that all publishers utilizing AdSense ads must comply with the Google AdSense Online Standard Terms and Conditions, and any accompanying policies, including content policies.

Do I need to update my SDK or make any code changes?

Publishers using a recent version of the SDK will not have to update their code. However, it's always a good idea to update to the most recent version. The latest version of our SDK can be found by clicking the "Manage Settings" button under your app's name in the Sites & Apps tab and following the "Get Publisher Code" link.

Can I serve Google ads and ads from Google certified ad networks on my mobile website?

No. It is only available in iOS and Android applications.

How are ad networks selected by Google?

We conduct a thorough certification process to ensure that ad networks meet Google's requirements for third-party ad serving with regard to user privacy, accuracy of measurement, latency, and compliance with our creative policies. At this time, we're focusing on our partners and vendors that have been specifically requested by our publishers.

What types of ads will appear if I enable Google ads and ads from Google certified ad networks?

Some ads will be the same text ads and click-to-call ads as those currently offered by Google. They will retain the "Ads by Google" branding. Here is an example Google ad:

In addition to Google ads, we will also offer image ads served by Google certified ad networks.

What are the content guidelines for Google ads? How can I ensure no inappropriate ads are shown in my app?

All ads that will be shown in your application comply with the Google AdWords ad format policies.

Can I filter or manage the AdSense ads that run in my application? Do the existing filters I set for my application apply to AdSense ads?

No, at this time you are not able to apply any filters on the content or type of AdSense ads that run inside your application.

How will I be paid?

You will be paid with a single check that includes all revenue generated by AdMob, Google, and Google certified ads in your application.

How will the Google ads be targeted?

The Google ads are targeted similarly to AdMob ads and based on the device, operator, location, type of application, etc. In addition, some Google ads are contextually targeted based on the description of the application.

Which publishers will benefit the most from this new feature?

Like all mobile advertising, the performance of ads will vary from application to application. However, applications with lower fill rates on the AdMob network should benefit the most from the additional ad inventory.

By taking the time to set up ad networks you'll be opening your app up to expanded revenue possibilities and also increasing its chances of ranking high on the user charts. Don't ignore this very important aspect of your growing app business!

Key Points to Remember from Chapter Five

- ✓ Developer accounts allow you to create and sell multiple apps across different platforms.
- ✓ Setting up analytics is an important aspect of running a successful app business.
- ✓ When you can track and review metrics on a daily basis you can make important changes to your app that could significantly impact your revenues.
- ✓ Use advertising networks to even further boost the revenue opportunities for your apps.

Chapter Six:

App Marketing and Promotion

The "build it and they will come" philosophy doesn't work in business, and it certainly doesn't work in the mobile app world. With so many options right at their fingertips today's consumers need to be *enticed* into trying a new app. As the owner, it's up to you to bring these willing buyers to your door through a multi-faceted marketing and advertising approach that we'll describe in this chapter.

Some of the strategies will be free, some will cost a few bucks, and others will be more expensive. Early on you'll probably opt for the strategies that are at the lower end of the cost scale. You'll work your way up from there by adding some of the "pay" options, testing them out, and then deciding if they are worth your investment.

We'll look first at how leverage mobile app store marketing and optimization to your advantage.

Mobile App Store Marketing & Optimization

Mobile App Store Marketing & Optimization is the mobile version of search engine optimization or SEO. In the world of website development this occurs when you use site content to get the attention of search engines like Google (instead of using pay-per-click or some other advertising method).

Think of the Apple iTunes store, the Blackberry store, and the Android marketplace as search engines that are dedicated to mobile apps. Making your app visible and ensuring that the sites' engines rank it as high as possible will be your top two goals. In fact, these strategies will be crucial to your app marketing plan.

The mobile app stores use different variables to figure out where to rank the apps that are sold through their channels. The Android market, for example, uses these key variables:

- ✓ Image: A poorly designed app thumbnail could ruin your app's odds of success.
- ✓ App name: Keep it short and to the point.
- ✓ Company name: Does it fit the app?
- ✓ Price: Maximize your chances of profitability by pricing your app correctly.
- ✓ Reviews: Good feedback equals more downloads.

When developing your optimization strategy you'll want to focus on the biggest app stores (Apple is by far the largest with more than 200,000 offerings). When writing your description, consider the people who will scan it. Since most people won't read an app description (especially if the app is free), you'll want to use pictures and bullet points to communicate the features and benefits.

Pay attention to the keywords that customers will type into their "search" bars in the app stores. Try to figure out which ones people will be most apt to type in when looking for your app and then make sure that those terms appear in as many places as possible within your app's page (much like you would do with web SEO).

There are some great ways to market your app successfully without breaking the bank. Here are 11 great starting points that you can test out in your own business:

1. **Share using AddThis:** You can increase your traffic and page rank with an "AddThis" button. Install it on your website or blog and ask visitors to share your content with their friends via Facebook, LinkedIn or one of the many other social networking sites.
2. **Q&A Sessions:** Participate in targeted app topic-specific discussions on LinkedIn Answers, WikiAnswers and other sites that allow you to become a trusted participant by providing answers to others.
3. **Use the Tell-a-friend in-app feature:** Add a conspicuous "Tell a friend" feature to your app. Using the consumer's personal contacts directory (for text messaging or email), you can send out messages that praise your app and provide a link where the recipient can learn more.
4. **Utilize Twitter's in-app feature:** Develop a Twitter update feature that allows users to tweet about how great your app is.
5. **Create a Facebook fan page:** Showcase your new app on a free fan page that's easy to set up and maintain.
6. **Offer a free trial:** Create a free trial version that gives users the option to gain more functionalities and/or eliminate advertising with the paid version.
7. **"App" up your email signature:** Create a signature line

that describes your app (and links to it) and use it in all of your emails.

8. **Social networking:** Tell friends, associates, and connections about your app on Twitter, LinkedIn, Facebook, and other social networking sites.

9. **Search directory registration:** List your app in free online directories such as DMOZ, an open directory service for sites like Google.

10. **Promote your app on a blog:** Use free platforms like WordPress or Blogger to blog about your app and to post useful news and information for readers. Integrate your blog into LinkedIn, Twitter, and Facebook.

11. **Continually improve your app:** One of the best ways to get new customers is by keeping your current users happy and up to date. Make fixes, add features, and take other steps to keep your app relevant.

There are dozens of other ways that you can promote your app. What creative strategies can you come up with?

App Websites & QR codes

Two additional marketing strategies you'll want to work into your business plan are app websites and QR codes. Here's a rundown of each and some thoughts on how to use them to your advantage:

App Websites

A website is a great strategy to pre-market and showcase your app. Be sure to include screenshots along with the features and benefits of your app. It is always a great idea for prelaunch to collect people's emails or have them like your app through the Facebook like button. By having people "like" your page, your app will be posted to their Facebook page so their friends can check out your app.

Use Google Adwords to figure out which keywords will get you the most attention and work them into your website as content (be sure not to oversell – you want the Web search engines to see your site as "quality" and not just "quantity").

Use a button that says "Available in the App Store" to get site visitors to click and buy your app (once it's released). You can also add a feedback feature where customers can discuss your app. Moderate requests and use the feedback when creating new versions of your app.

QR Codes

First developed in Japan in 1994, these high-density, two-dimensional marketing tools are basically just barcodes that are comprised of spots instead of bars. Those "spots" come together to make up codes, which in turn house the data that's scanned by mobile devices. The devices quickly scan and digest the code's information block, translating it into hyperlinks or text information.

QR codes are being used across a wide variety of advertising mediums – from magazine ads to postcards to billboards. They allow for easy tracking of offline marketing efforts, provide a new channel for direct sales, and help stretch advertising dollars. You can use QR codes to help consumers go through the process of selecting and purchasing your app very quickly. For example, if you embed QR codes in the reviews about your apps, the user can hit the code with their barcode reader and be whisked off to the download section of the Android or Apple app market. And while QR codes are still catching on in the mainstream, they provide an easy and direct way to get tech-savvy consumers interested in – and purchasing – your apps.

Video Marketing

Video marketing is hot right now and YouTube is the clear leader. In fact, YouTube is the #2 search engine after Google, making it an especially attractive choice for app owners who are looking for free advertising for their products.

To get started you'll want to set up a free account and then create a short clip about your new app. In the clip you'll want to focus on the features, benefits, and ease of use. Make users want to learn more and give them a direct link to the app store(s) where your product can be downloaded.

Don't stop at just one video. Set up a YouTube Channel where you can showcase all of your videos. Use highly targeted terms to tag every video and use YouTube's analytics tools to figure out how many people are viewing your clips (you can look at visitors by demographic and popularity).

If you want to invest a few dollars in your online video campaign, purchase a sponsored ad (through Google AdWords) that promotes your app video. These ads will appear in the YouTube search results along the right side of the page.

Moving pictures are all the rage online right now. Why not tap into this excellent marketing opportunity and use it to stretch your advertising dollars even further?

Getting Reviews and Ratings

It's no secret that the Internet has become one gigantic sounding board for anyone and everyone to talk about everything. Whether it's the news of the day, celebrity gossip, or the newest piece of technology – you can read about it online, and then see what everyone else (or at least those folks who take the time to comment) has to say about it.

You can use this to your advantage by getting customers, bloggers, journalists, and other individuals to test out your app and provide feedback about it.

Bloggers are a good place to start. These folks need great stuff to write about and your app could easily be one of their topics for the week. Check out the blogs that are most closely aligned with the audience you're trying to reach (gaming blogs for gamers, business blogs for productivity tools, and so forth) and find out what their guidelines are for submissions and correspondence. Each blog has a different process; some bloggers have an email address to send submissions to, while others use a web form on their site. Make it easy on the recipient by providing, along with your introductory email or form submission:

- ✓ Your app's name
- ✓ App category
- ✓ Company name
- ✓ Short overview of your app with key features and benefits highlighted (without going overboard)
- ✓ A direct link to app
- ✓ A promotional code (if it's a paid app)
- ✓ Current rank/highest rank achieved (if applicable)
- ✓ Release date

Be sure to include screenshots, videos, icons, and other graphics with your submission. Upload large files to Dropbox or Photobucket so that you don't overload the recipient's email server.

Shhh…Insider App Secret!

If you're about to launch a brand new, innovative app consider giving reviewers an exclusive "first look" at the product. Make the recipients feel as if they are getting an  exclusive and the odds that they'll read your email and respond positively will be much higher!

Once one or more parties have reviewed your app you can use the positive feedback in several ways, including:

- ✓ Mention it in your app description
- ✓ Share the link to the review with as many people as possible
- ✓ Post links to the review and/or mention it in your marketing materials
- ✓ Put the reviewer on your list for future apps!

App Review Websites

There are sites that are dedicated to reviewing new apps. Some of the leading ones are:

- ✓ AppCraver
- ✓ 148apps
- ✓ AppVee
- ✓ iPhoneAppReviews.net
- ✓ Apple iPhone School

- ✓ AppStoreApps.com
- ✓ iPhoneApplicationList
- ✓ TUAW
- ✓ Apps Safari

Shhh....Insider App Secret!

Remember that these review websites index well in the search engines and as a result can drive traffic to download your apps, both short-term and long term. Think about the keyword terms that you want to list in your review, both for users and for the search engines.

Here are the home pages for a few of these sites so that you can see how they are laid out and what they typically cover:

AppCraver

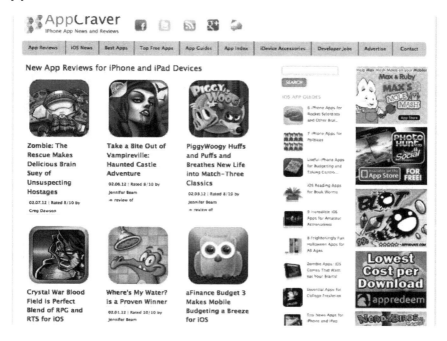

148Apps

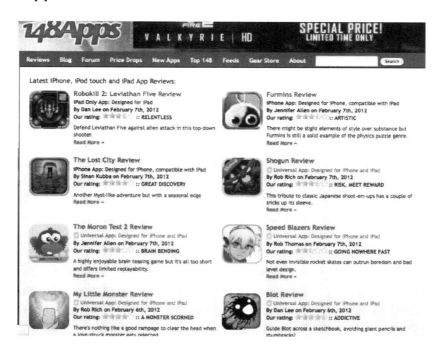

App Safari

The process for submitting to app review sites is pretty straightforward:

- ✓ Submit your app for review.
- ✓ Provide a promo code so that the editorial staff can review your app without having to pay for it.
- ✓ Follow up as needed.

You now have a full arsenal of marketing strategies and probably a few more good ideas of your own. In the next chapter we'll look at the various revenue models that you can use when developing and selling apps, and show you how to turn your business into a profitable venture.

Shhh....Insider App Secret!

Fast track your app submissions by using our App Submitter tool. In less than five minutes you can submit your app to over 200 websites. Visit:

www.HowToMakeMillionsFromApps.com/AppSubmitter

Key Points to Remember from Chapter Six

- ✓ There are a lot of effective, inexpensive ways to market your app to the masses.
- ✓ You can use appstore SEO much like you would use SEO online for website marketing.
- ✓ Video marketing on YouTube is one free way to get exposure for your apps.
- ✓ Bloggers, journalists, and customers are all good sources of positive reviews and feedback that you can use to promote your apps.

Chapter Seven:
Monetizing Your Apps

I've talked about the financial opportunities associated with mobile apps in every chapter of this book, and in one format or another. Now it's time to look more carefully at the top ways to monetize an app and put some money in your pocket. There are several ways that you can do this and they range from paid apps to freemium options to in-app advertising, and everything in between.

We'll kick things off by looking at in-app transactions as a monetization method and then work our way through the rest of the options.

In-App Transactions

To generate revenues through in-app transactions, you'll want to offer up a free app that users know, love, and trust. These folks will be most apt to make in-app purchases of upgrades, other services, new versions, and so forth.

Put simply, you'll hook them with your great app and then ask them to pay for the additional services. If they love your app they will go for it and voila, you'll be generating money as an app owner.

Shhh.....Insider App Secret!

Integrate social networking into your app and the odds users will tell their friends about it will rise, thus enhancing your in-app transactions – and for little

or no advertising dollars! Make sure you use the Open Graph API's and test what it looks like when a post is made to the social networks. You don't want to spam people's walls, you want your posts to be engaging. Check the images, from urls, titles and short descriptions. This is where you can have some fun and show personality. See if you can change and adapt the message so it is not always the say.

One poker app, for example, sells users play-money chips with an in-app chip store. This store is the app's main revenue generator. When users run out of chips they have to buy more in order to keep playing. This is what traditional marketers would call a "continuity program," and it's just one of many ways you can develop a consistent revenue stream with in-app transactions.

Freemium Model

Nearly 90 percent of the top-ranked iOS 250 applications worldwide are free to download and ABI Research expects that number to increase in 2012. In the U.S., that number is just 10 percent, but is also expected to rise over the next few years.

What does this mean for app owners? It means you'll have to be creative when it comes to finding a sustainable revenue stream from your apps. Consumers love free stuff and once they know that most of the top apps are free, they'll gravitate to those models over the "pay upfront" options.

One way to do this is to use "freemium" apps. These models give the app itself away for free, and then offer customers various game or app enhancements that can't be accessed and used without paying a fee.

The freemium model is popular on mobile phones and on iPads. It gives away its core functionality for free and offers upgrades to add certain features and very often combines the "lite" version of an app with "full" version. The latter can be unlocked using an in-app purchase.

At its core, the freemium model is based on the principle that once a customer downloads your app and finds it useful he or she will spend money to upgrade to expanded models, purchase additional credits, or take some other step that results in a revenue generating event.

Paid Apps

The most obvious way to make money from mobile apps is by selling them for a fee. iPhone apps are sold in increments of a dollar starting at $0.99 ($0.99, $1.99, $2.99, etc.). Apple takes 30 percent of each sale, which means a $0.99 application will net you $0.69. Sounds minimal right? Well multiply it over thousands of downloads and the profits will definitely add up.

Just ask Lima Sky, the developer of the popular game Doodle Jump. The app sells for under $1 and netted over $2 million in revenues during its first 12 months on the market.

There are pros and cons to offering paid apps, including:

Pros: The income potential is high. The App Store favors paid apps over free ones (since they don't generate money off of free apps). If your app sells well you'll have a predictable income source.

Cons: Users have to be willing to upfront for your app (which means it better be good!). The app store may take a significant cut of your revenues. You'll need good exposure in the app store in order to increase your app's sales.

Do your research before deciding whether to offer a paid or free app. Check out what other developers in your category are doing and then come up with a price point (free or otherwise) that's well-suited for your particular app.

Shhh.....Insider App Secret!

Create a free version of your app to get people downloading and addicted to your app and then move them into a purchasing environment. The app needs to show people it is worth paying. Also consider creating a premium version of your app – with all of the features – for free. When the app – which is priced at $4.99 to $9.99 – sells, there will be more profits in the sale.

In-App Advertising

Putting "ads in apps" is a great way to monetize mobile apps and to start generating revenue through alternative channels. If your app already has a big audience – and if it's a targeted demographic – even better. Your app will be an especially attractive target for advertisers, and it will serve as a solid revenue generator for your portfolio.

Now, you could negotiate with individual companies to place ads within your app or to do a product placement. Or, you could work with one of the dozens of online advertising firms that serve as "intermediaries" between app developers and advertisers. These firms act much like Google does with its AdSense program for websites: you sign up and the advertising firm selects and feeds the appropriate ads to your app.

If you decide to put ads in your app you'll have to offer the product for free, since consumers won't stand for ads and upfront fees. It's really one or the other. Weigh out the pros and cons of each option and figure out the best approach for your specific situation.

In the last chapter of this book we'll talk about the sales potential of your app business and show you how to develop an effective exit strategy for your company.

Key Points to Remember from Chapter Seven

- ✓ Free apps are popular, but certain paid apps generate a tremendous amount of revenue for their owners.
- ✓ In-app purchases are a great way to turn a free app into a revenue-generating model.
- ✓ The freemium model is used often to generate money with free apps.
- ✓ You can use in-app ads to boost revenues without having to charge for your app or related upgrades and premium services.

Chapter Eight:
Cashing Out

Regardless of what type of business you are starting, or what products/services you're selling, you should always start with the end in mind. Even if you are just starting to dip your toe into the mobile app pool you should be thinking about an exit strategy and how you'll execute when the time comes.

App businesses are becoming high attractive to investor, but you need to make sure you have spent the time to document your success and failures. Also make sure you have made the transition process simple (for example, by setting up a company-owned developer account) so the company can be sold.

Ensure you financials are up to date and that you can show downloads, revenues, income streams on charts. Create a sales document that outlines how attractive your business is to purchase. Also highlight some of the things that can be done to increase its revenues over the next 12 months.

Here are some of the revenue drivers to highlight:
- Localization of the apps into additional languages
- Expand platforms to Android and Amazon
- Integrate social media
- Add additional advertising to apps through NAG Screens, push notifications, offer walls or affiliate links

Your potential buyers will want to know that they have access to developers, source codes and graphic assets for the apps. When selling app portfolios, for example, I create a hosting account and a website in the name of my app portfolio account.

Creating a website when you launch a new developer account positions the portfolio for sale and makes me look more serious and professional. In the hosting account I securely load all of the app source codes, graphical assets, videos and related documents. The easier you can make the sale the more likely a purchaser is to spend money with you.

If you take the time to make your developer account attractive to a buyer, then someone will buy it. This is one of the reasons I publish press releases and link them to my websites. It creates credibility and trust, and makes people want to work with me.

Exit plans are also important. According to the U.S. Small Business Administration (SBA), very few business owners have exit and/or succession plans in place. If you decide that selling your business is the right exit strategy for you, be sure that you cover all your bases.

In order to sell your business officially, you will need to prepare a sales agreement. This is the key document in buying the business assets or stock of a corporation. It is important to make sure the agreement is accurate and contains all the terms of the purchase. It would be a good idea to have an attorney review this document. It is in this agreement that you should define everything that you intend to purchase of the business, assets, customer lists, intellectual property and goodwill.

The SBA suggests using this checklist of items that should be addressed in the agreement:

- ✓ Names of seller, buyer, and business
- ✓ Background information
- ✓ Assets being sold
- ✓ Purchase price and Allocation of Assets
- ✓ Covenant Not to Compete
- ✓ Any adjustments to be made
- ✓ The Terms of the Agreement and payment terms
- ✓ List of inventory included in the sale
- ✓ Any representation and warranties of the seller and buyer
- ✓ Determination as to the access to any business information
- ✓ Determination as to the running of the business prior to closing
- ✓ Contingencies
- ✓ Fees, including brokers fees
- ✓ Date of closing

For more information on "Getting Out" of your business visit the SBA online at: http://www.sba.gov/category/navigation-structure/starting-managing-business/managing-business/getting-out

Another way to unload your app business is by working with a business broker that specializes in the business. One such company outlines the process used to match up app business sellers and buyers as:

1. Fill out a form detailing your business and goals.
2. Get an evaluation of the best plan that fits your goals

3. Set up a short confidential phone call to discuss your business.
4. Obtain a free estimated valuation of your business.
5. Market the listing to a database of qualified buyers.
6. Locate additional qualified buyers to make sure you get the best deal.

This broker charges no upfront fees and receives a "success fee" (negotiated in advance) once the company is sold.

If you plan to work with a broker be sure to go over the sales process and fees <u>before</u> signing any contracts or sealing any deals. You may also want to consult with an attorney or an accountant during the process.

Here are a few more exit strategies you'll want to start using now, before you even launch your first app:

1) Start by treating your business like a business, rather than a solo enterprise. This single step will put you far ahead of many other app owners, whose businesses are closely tied to their own personal performance and success.

2) Document all processes (no matter how insignificant they may seem) that you, your assistant(s) and team members use during the course of business.

3) Maintain accurate and complete financial records to prove your business' value.

4)   Don't wait until the month before you retire to begin taking these steps. Whether you're 20, 50 or 75, the time is now to begin thinking about how to make a smooth exit from the business that you're going to put time, money and effort into.

Ready, Set, Go!

Congratulations! You've reached the end of this book. We truly hope that you'll come away knowing what it takes to make millions in the mobile app arena – a venue where you can generate a tidy sum every month by coming up with innovative, useful apps for the masses. We wish you good luck in your venture!

If you want more information, visit us at: www.HowToMakeMillionsWithApps.Com. You will find additional tools and resources, plus all of the training you need to be successful when creating, publishing and marketing apps.

On our blog you'll find hours of videos that answer questions and provide useful tips and strategies for increasing the revenues that you generate from your apps.

Key Points to Remember from Chapter Eight

- ✓ Have an exit strategy in mind before you go into the app business.
- ✓ Treat your business like a business – not a hobby.
- ✓ By maintaining accurate financial records you'll be able to justify the valuation of your company.
- ✓ You can work with an app business broker to find qualified buyers quickly.

Chapter Nine:

Resources for App Developers

Here you will find the information on the bonuses available with this book. To access your bonuses all you need to do is visit www.HowToMakeMillionsFromApps.com/BookMembers

Bonus #1 - How To Create Apps Blueprint + 45 Minute Video Introduction

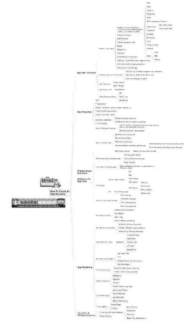

The step-by-step blueprint that I personally use to create apps, day after day. I have even trained my developers, designers, and virtual assistants to use this document to manage each step of the process. This Blueprint is something you will want to print out, put up on your wall, and use as a roadmap.

Benjamin personally walks you through this entire blueprint to make sure that you understand the elements and to help you get started today.

Bonus #2 - Non-Disclosure Agreement Template (NDA)

Protect your app idea with this NDA agreement template that you can use right now, whenever you speak to anyone about your app idea. That's right: When you share you idea, speak to designers or developers you want to ensure they do not steal your idea and profit from it themselves.

Bonus #3 – IP Ownership With Independent Contractor Agreement.

 One of the fatal mistake people make when engaging graphic designers, coders, programmers, or other third parties is <u>not</u> securing their Intellectual Property Rights (IP). All rights must transfer to you, and not remain with your contractor. Save yourself from being sued, or having to pay thousands of dollars in royalty fees, by completing this template today and using it with everyone you work with.

Bonus #4 – Software Development Agreement

 This simple agreement will save you time and money and make it easy to protect your money and app idea. Save yourself hundreds of dollars in legal fees by using this template with your contractors. Get your app development clearly defined – from payment milestones to what your outsourcers are actually building for you.

When you visit the blog and members' area you'll also have gain access to hours of videos lessons personally developed by Benjamin.

What are you waiting for you? Instantly access your bonuses and more by visiting:
www.HowToMakeMillionsFromApps.com/BookMembers

Discover the secrets of creating, publishing and marketing apps with no coding, programming or design experience.

*The complete system for creating, publishing and marketing apps with over **$1,882 worth of bonuses**.*

App Success System

Module 1- How To Find An Underserved Market And Position Yourself To Capitalize On It

- Zeroing-in on profitable niches and serving them apps that they'll download like crazy

- The ins and outs of getting your account approved with every major app store

- Leaping over the inner workings of the app stores so you can move quickly and get your ideas to market *faster*

Module 2- How To CASH IN BIG With Every App Idea

- How to make windfall profits, even with free apps

- Using the hidden information in the App Purchase checklist to create a treasure trove of revenue

- How to leverage the top 25 app charts for a mountain of money

Module 3- Never Before Revealed FREE Sources For Making Apps Now

- How to slap a crowd-pleasing app together with no coding or programming knowledge

- Little known techniques for using Word Press to create an app

- Classified list of resources for making your app for FREE

Module 4- How To Find, Recruit, Hire & Manage Your Virtual Production Team

- The best places to outsource and how to snag top notch developers, even with a small budget

- Keeping tabs of your virtual development team even while you sleep

- How to avoid costly mistakes that will save you a ton of cash and speed your app development

Module 5- How To Be A Highly-Paid Business App Consultant And Bank A Vault Of Cash

- The surefire local business door opener that will have them standing in line for your new apps

- Add-on products and services you can market to pull a boatload of revenue from every transaction

- The fast and inexpensive app-building process that helps you create a money machine

Module 6- Data Mining App Analytics For Hidden Payoffs

- FREE tracking analytics that unlock a roadmap to riches

- Value-added app tracking and how to profit from it

Module 7- How To Unleash Your Apps To Lucrative And Hungry Markets

- Three unknown tricks for boosting your downloads the day your app launches…and everyday thereafter

- App store confidential information you can use to optimize everything you do for maximum return

- Where to go to get people to review your app and blast your downloads into the top 20

Module 8 - The Art And Science Of App Website Magnets

- How to get your app website built in record time for pennies on the dollar

- The advantage of QR codes and how to use them to multiply your downloads like magic

- A mega-list of resources to put you ahead of every app developer on the planet

This easy to follow, progressive blueprint will put you on a level playing field and years ahead of anyone developing apps today!

Cash in on the Apps Gold Rush with the App Success System.

As soon as you download you'll have everything you need to…

- Start your app army with a single foot soldier and then **rocket to a battalion of apps** that will deliver more monthly income than most people earn in a year

- Circle yourself with expert developers **you can hire for less than a month's rent on an apartment**

- **Outpace every app in production** and hurdle the top download list as if you owned the list yourself

Create a money-machine and have more fun than you've ever had in your life

Our 3O Day 100% Money Back Guarantee

Here's your UNCONDITIONAL GUARANTEE— download the entire program and use it for a full 30 days, one month...

...if after those 4 weeks you are not 100% completely satisfied, you can cancel and get a **FULL NO QUESTIONS ASKED REFUND.** You don't even have to send anything back.

I'm taking all the risk here, because I know once you get into this course and light bulbs start to fire, you'll be app happy.

Order your copy of the App Success System today to start fast tracking your app success. It is easier than you think to make money from apps. Visit www.AppSuccessSystem.com, call our office +1 702 430 1909, or Fax your order form to +1 888 573 0556.

FAX ORDER FORM +1 888 573 0556

Credit Card Type :   Visa   AMEX   Master Card   Discover

Credit Card Number: _____

Expiry: __ /__Signature:_____

Name:_____

Address:_____

City:_____State:_____ZIP:_____

Country:_____ Phone:_____

Email:_____

Courses Offered at www.HowToMakeMillionsWithApps.com

Mobile App Success System

7-week program to build your App Portfolio. Starting from ground zero you will be provided with the complete blueprint for creating, publishing and marketing apps on Apple IOS, Android, Amazon Marketplace, Windows and Html 5. You will know the style of apps you need to build, how to get them built, and how to market them.

App Legends Program

9-week Personalized Program for building your complete app business. Fast track your success with Benjamin's App Source Codes + Custom Built Social App Software. If you want to know the secrets to building social apps that are downloaded by millions of people, this is the program for you. You will have a 12-month blueprint that includes and exit strategy to sell your app portfolio, should you choose to. You will discover Benjamin's personal secrets to how selling app portfolios ranging from $50,000 to $300,000. This program is offered by invitation only, operated twice a year, and includes a live event for all current program members.

App Marketing and Consulting Packages

Contact the Tigga Studios office if you would like to book App Marketing, App Development or Consulting packages. Call our office on USA +1 702 403 1909 and speak with our team today. www.TiggaStudios.com

24757445R00085

Made in the USA
Middletown, DE
05 October 2015